SCIENTISTS

LINUS PAULING

ADVANCING SCIENCE, ADVOCATING PEACE

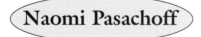

Naomi Pasachoff

Enslow Publishers, Inc.

40 Industrial Road   PO Box 38
Box 398   Aldershot
Berkeley Heights, NJ 07922   Hants GU12 6BP
USA   UK

http://www.enslow.com

"My career has been unique. . . . Perhaps one person in a million . . . can be said to have led a life that differs as much from that of most other human beings."

—Linus Pauling

Dedication
In loving memory of Milton R. Konvitz (1908–2003)
and of Florence Aptekar (1911–2003)

Library of Congress Cataloging-in-Publication Data

Pasachoff, Naomi E.
    Linus Pauling : advancing science, advocating peace / Naomi Pasachoff.
        p. cm. — (Nobel Prize-winning scientists)
    Summary: Profiles the Nobel Prize-winning chemist who described the nature of chemical bonds, made important discoveries in the fields of quantum mechanics, immunology, and evolution, and used his scientific fame to help advance political causes.
    Includes bibliographical references and index.
    ISBN 0-7660-2130-0
    1. Pauling, Linus, 1901—Juvenile literature. 2. Chemists—United States—Biography—Juvenile literature. [1. Pauling, Linus, 1901- 2. Chemists. 3. Scientists. 4. Nobel prizes—Biography.] I. Title. II. Series.
    QD22.P35P37 2004
    540'.92—dc21

                                                    2003006475

Printed in the United States of America

10 9 8 7 6 5 4 3 2 1

To Our Readers:
We have done our best to make sure all Internet Addresses in this book were active and appropriate when we went to press. However, the author and the publisher have no control over and assume no liability for the material available on those Internet sites or on other Web sites they may link to. Any comments or suggestions can be sent by e-mail to comments@enslow.com or to the address on the back cover.

Every effort has been made to locate all copyright holders of material used in this book. If any errors or omissions have occurred, corrections will be made in future editions of this book.

Illustration Credits: © The Nobel Foundation, p. 5; Courtesy Ava Helen and Linus Pauling Papers, Oregon State University Special Collections, p. 68; Courtesy of the Archives, California Institute of Technology, pp. 53, 92; National Library of Medicine, p. 18; Photo by Robert Cohen/Courtesy Caltech Archives, p. 81; Pressens Bild, p. 12; The Ball Studio, p. 33.

Cover Illustration: Donald Jenkins/National Library of Medicine (foreground); Kenneth Eward/BioGrafx/Photo Researchers, Inc. (background).

CONTENTS

ACKNOWLEDGMENTS

I wish to take this opportunity to express my thanks to a number of people who assisted me in preparing this book.

A number of librarians at Williams College provided invaluable assistance, including Alison O'Grady, Interlibrary Loan Supervisor; Helena F. Warburg, Head of the Schow Science Library; and members of their staffs.

Several scientists read drafts of the manuscript at different stages and offered helpful comments. They include Dr. Alfred Goldberg, Professor of Cell Biology, Harvard Medical School; Dr. Raymond Chang, Professor of Natural Sciences, Williams College; and Dr. Charles M. Lovett, Professor of Chemistry, Williams College.

Members of the Pauling family were also good enough to share their suggestions for improving the manuscript. They include Pauling's oldest son and namesake, Dr. Linus Pauling, Jr.; Pauling's daughter, Linda Pauling Kamb; and her husband, Barclay Kamb, Professor of Geology and Geophysics, Emeritus, California Institute of Technology.

I would also like to thank Judith R. Goodstein, University Archivist, Institute Archives, California Institute of Technology. With her guidance, I spent a very interesting day at Caltech visiting various Pauling-related sites.

My husband, as always, was my first and most critical reader. My daughters, Eloise and Deborah, and Eloise's husband, Tom Glaisyer, cheerfully listened to my endless talk of Pauling during the months of research, thus helping me focus the coverage of the book.

Despite the helpful input of all these individuals, however, if any errors remain in the book, I alone am responsible for them.

Naomi Pasachoff

THE NOBEL PRIZE

Almost every year since its founding in 1901, the Nobel Prize has been awarded to individuals who have distinguished themselves in the fields of physiology or medicine, physics, chemistry, literature, and peace. (In 1968 a prize for economics was added.) The prize is named for Alfred Nobel, a Swede born in Stockholm in 1833, who grew up to become a successful chemist, manufacturer, and businessman.

Nobel began experimenting with ways to make nitroglycerine, an explosive, safer for practical use. Eventually he found a way to make a paste of nitroglycerine mixed with silica. He could then shape the paste into a stick that could be placed in holes drilled in rocks. He patented this creation in 1867 and named it dynamite. In order to detonate the dynamite sticks, Nobel also invented a blasting cap that could be ignited by burning a fuse. The invention of dynamite, along with equipment like the diamond drilling crown and the pneumatic drill, significantly reduced the expenses associated with many types of construction work.

Soon Nobel's dynamite and blasting caps were in great demand. Nobel proved to be an astute businessman, establishing companies and laboratories throughout the world. He also continued to experiment with other chemical inventions and held more than 350 patents in his lifetime.

Alfred Nobel did not narrow his learning to scientific knowledge alone. His love of literature and poetry prompted him to write his own works, and his social conscience kept him interested in peace-related issues.

When Nobel died on December 10, 1896, and his will was read, everyone was surprised to learn that he left instructions for the accumulated fortune from his companies and business ventures (estimated at more than $3 million U.S.) to be used to award prizes in physics, chemistry, physiology or medicine, literature, and peace.

In fulfilling Alfred Nobel's will, the Nobel Foundation was established in order to oversee the funds left by Nobel and to coordinate the work of the prize-awarding institutions. Nobel prizes are presented every December 10, the anniversary of Alfred Nobel's death.

CHAPTER ONE

A LAUREATE RESPECTED AND SUSPECTED

On November 3, 1954, chemist Linus Pauling was preparing to give a seminar talk at Cornell University in Ithaca, New York. A lecture by Pauling—a gifted public speaker—was always well attended. But today's lecture was preceded by unexpected news that turned it into a real event.

Minutes before the talk, Pauling received a phone call from a reporter. Pauling had just been selected to receive that year's Nobel Prize for chemistry. The Swedish Nobel Committee was honoring him "for research into the nature of the chemical bond . . . and its application to the elucidation of complex substances." Over a period of more than twenty years, Pauling had helped explain how the matter that makes up everything in the universe is held together. He made use of his unusual background in physics and mathematics as well as chemistry to explain the forces by which atoms are bound in a molecule or crystal. He had recently shed light on the structure of the proteins that are necessary for the chemical processes that occur in living organisms.

As the news of the Nobel Prize spread, first around campus and then around the world, Pauling was widely congratulated. Colleagues not only at Cornell, where he was a visiting lecturer, but also at other institutions expressed their delight. At the California Institute of Technology, the delight was shared by administrators, faculty, and staff. Pauling was one of them. He had come to Caltech (as the famous scientific institution is widely known) as a graduate student in 1922, had joined the faculty in 1927, and had been head of its division of chemistry and chemical engineering since 1937. A month after the great news was announced, a large party was held at Caltech. Over 350 guests honored Caltech's star.

Like other recipients of the Nobel Prize, Pauling was expected to attend the awards ceremony in Stockholm, Sweden, and to present a lecture on his prizewinning work. The ceremonies were to begin on December 10, 1954.

But would Pauling be permitted to attend? Why should the question even arise? The answer had to do not with science but with politics. For nearly a decade, Pauling had been an outspoken critic of the United States' Cold War policies. (The Cold War was the state of political tension that characterized U.S. relations with the Soviet Union after World War II ended in 1945. Because the situation did not lead to widespread actual fighting, or "hot" war, it remained a "cold war.") Pauling called for peaceful relations with the

Soviet Union. In particular he criticized the continued development and testing of nuclear weapons by each side.

During the early 1950s, Americans who expressed such views were often suspected of disloyalty to their country. Many people considered the Soviet Union and its allies as a threat to everything that made America great. After all, the American dream, where anyone could rise from rags to riches, was possible only under capitalism. Capitalism is the economic system based on private ownership, where working hard can be the key to wealth. Such self-advancement was not possible under communism, the system that underlay the economic, political, and social life of the Soviet Union. Under communism, the government runs the economy. In theory, the long-range goal of communism is a society providing equality and economic security for all. In practice, however, the government was a dictatorship. Members of the Communist Party—the only permitted political party—had privileges that were denied to nonmembers.

Because Pauling's political views made him suspect, the U.S. State Department denied him on more than one occasion the passport necessary for foreign travel. In this instance he was not granted a passport until November 27, 1954. The Pauling family barely made it to Stockholm in time for the ceremonies.

So Pauling was able to give his Nobel speech on "Modern Structural Chemistry." He explained that the key to advancements in science is understanding the way atoms hold together in molecules and in specific structures. He concluded with the prediction that "the chemist of the future. . .will come to rely upon a new structural chemistry, involving precise geometrical relationships among the atoms and the molecules." He also predicted that "great progress will be made, through this technique, in the attack, by chemical methods, on the problems of biology and medicine."[1]

Pauling thus came close to being prevented by his own government from receiving in person the world's most prestigious award. He did not, however, conclude from his brush with the authorities that he should refrain from speaking out on political matters. Instead, he decided that his celebrity made it even more of a responsibility to speak his mind on the best way to achieve world peace.

On December 10, 1963, the Nobel Peace Committee, based in Oslo, Norway, announced that Linus Pauling had been awarded the Nobel Peace prize for 1962 for his efforts to ban nuclear weapons. (After issuing no award during 1962, the committee announced two awards in 1963.) Pauling was the first—and so far only—person ever to win two unshared Nobel prizes.

Congratulatory messages reached Pauling from around the world. Yet at Caltech his achievement was ignored or questioned. The institute gave him no party to rival the one of nine years earlier. A few supportive colleagues in the biology division hastily threw together a small affair. Meanwhile, the U.S. government and the media also showed little approval of Pauling's new honor. On their arrival at the Oslo airport, the Pauling family

> *"Great progress will be made, through [a new structural chemistry] on the problems of biology and medicine."*
>
> —Linus Pauling

found no representative of the U.S. government on hand to welcome them. The U.S. embassy did not even throw the customary party in honor of the new laureate.

The coverage of the award in *The New York Herald Tribune* typified the hostile media response to Pauling. The paper ran an editorial titled "The Nobel Peacenik Prize." Peacenik was the derisive name given to people like Pauling who championed peace at a time when many thought only a strong military could secure the future of America. The editorial argued that "Award of the Nobel Peace Prize to Dr. Pauling . . . associates this . . . honor with the extravagant posturings of a placarding peacenik."[2]

However his institution and his country viewed the award, Pauling himself found it very satisfying. While doing his chemistry research had been a source of pure enjoyment for him, his peace work had taken up much time that he might otherwise have devoted to science. It was gratifying to have his scientific self-denial recognized in such an important way.

In his 1963 Nobel Lecture, "Science and Peace," Pauling said, "The world has been greatly changed, especially during the last century, by the discoveries of scientists." Although nuclear weapons were developed by scientists, "scientists have taken a leading part . . . in urging that vigorous action be taken to prevent the use of the new weapons and to abolish war from the world." He also spoke prophetically of the potential hazards of biological and chemical weapons. He called for "a general agreement to stop research and development of these weapons, to prohibit their use." Since use of any of these weapons could lead to the extinction of the human race, he spoke of the

LINUS PAULING (RIGHT) RECEIVES HIS 1954 CHEMISTRY PRIZE FROM KING GUSTAV VI OF SWEDEN ON DECEMBER 10, 1954.

need for "the abolition of war and its replacement by world law."[3]

To the end of his life, Pauling remained a controversial figure. For most of his last thirty years, he promoted his belief that large doses of vitamin C are vital for human health. He pursued this crusade despite the opposition of medical authorities who insisted there was no scientific proof to support his argument. Many considered him a dangerous crank. They worried that countless people would suffer if they followed Pauling's advice. In addition to having his loyalty suspected, Pauling now also found himself ridiculed for his health claims.

At the age of eighty (he lived to be ninety-three),

Pauling said, "My career has been unique. . . . Perhaps one person in a million, or one person in a hundred thousand, or one person in ten million, can be said to have led a life that differs as much from that of most other human beings as mine."[4] He was unique not only in being the first (and still only) person to receive two unshared Nobel prizes but also in coming close to being awarded a third, in medicine, for his discovery that inherited diseases can result from alterations in the structure of protein molecules. His career was also unique in evoking great controversy in addition to great respect.

No one could deny, however, the many significant contributions Pauling made over his very long life. Among the comments made by his colleagues after his death, the following is representative: "Although Pauling was often controversial and was sometimes criticized in both scientific and political arenas, it is incontrovertible that he had a major impact on science, education, and international peace."[5]

CHAPTER TWO

AN OREGON
BOYHOOD

Linus Carl Pauling was born on February 28, 1901, in Portland, Oregon. There was no reason to predict he would grow up to be the first person to win two unshared Nobel prizes. His father, Herman Henry William Pauling, the son of German immigrants, had dropped out of school in the tenth grade. Herman Pauling had then convinced a pharmacist in his hometown of Oswego, Oregon, to take him on as an apprentice. He thus learned to prepare the pills, ointments, and syrups used as medications.

Like his son after him, Herman Pauling was ambitious and hardworking. By the age of nineteen he had moved to Portland, where he worked in a number of large pharmacies. In 1899 a group of Portland investors sent him to start a pharmacy in the young but quickly growing frontier town of Condon, Oregon.

In May 1900 twenty-three-year-old Herman Pauling married nineteen-year-old Lucy Isabelle ("Belle") Darling, the second of four daughters of Linus Darling. When Belle

Darling was seven, her mother died after a difficult childbirth. About five years later, Linus Darling married a wealthy farmer's widow. As a daughter of one of the now wealthier and more respected citizens of Condon, Belle became quite spoiled.

Herman Pauling seemed to have excellent career prospects when Belle Darling married him. But shortly after the wedding, Herman lost his position as the Condon pharmacist. The young couple moved back to Portland, where he found a job with less prestige and lower income as a drug-supply company clerk. In their inexpensive apartment in a poor Portland neighborhood, Belle gave birth to the future Nobel laureate. By 1904, Linus had two younger sisters, Pauline and Frances Lucile.

Throughout his short life Herman Pauling did his best to earn the kind of living that would make his wife happy. By the time Linus was eight, the family had moved five times as Herman sought the best opportunities to make a living. In a childhood of many upheavals, Linus felt most secure in Condon. As a grown man, Pauling described what the town was like when his family moved there. "In 1905 my parents went to live in Condon, Oregon, on the eastern side of the Cascade Mountains, where my mother had grown up. The population of five hundred included mainly cowboys, ranch hands, and saloon keepers."[1] This time Herman Pauling's Condon pharmacy thrived, transforming him into one of the town's leading businessmen. He never liked the small town, however, and always viewed his pharmacy there as a stepping stone to a future business back in Portland.

Unfortunately, Herman Pauling would never fulfill his

business aspirations. In 1909 the Condon pharmacy was destroyed in a fire, and he moved his family back to Portland. There Herman was able to rent a fine family home and begin to establish his dream pharmacy. On June 11, 1910, however, he died suddenly, probably of a perforated stomach ulcer.

Linus Pauling never had a good relationship with his mother, who was not in tune with her son's intellectual nature. Pauling vaguely recalled, however, that his father "had been pretty interested in me." One incident stood out: "Some months before [my father's] death he wrote a letter to the Portland *Oregonian*, asking for advice as to what books he should get for his precocious [nine-year-old] son, who was an avid reader. 'Please don't suggest the Bible and Darwin's *The Origin of Species*,' he said, 'because he's already read these books.' He described me as being especially attracted to ancient history and natural science."[2]

In his response to Herman Pauling, the editor of the state's largest newspaper recommended works by the fifth-century B.C. Greek historian Herodotus, the later Greek biographer Plutarch, and the 19th-century English writer Matthew Arnold.

Although Pauling did not trace his interest in science back to his father, he recalled that "as a young boy I used to hang around his store. I remember watching him mix up different pharmaceutical concoctions for his customers and then put them into little bottles. Perhaps at that time I wanted to become a druggist myself; I can't remember what I thought. My father died when I was nine years old, so he couldn't have had a very great effect on me."[3]

But Herman Pauling's sudden death had a devastating

effect on his young family. Belle not only became deeply depressed but also soon began to suffer from pernicious anemia. There was no cure at the time for this severe blood disorder. Her mental and physical health were worsened by the dramatic change in the family's economic prospects. In order to raise the three children, who now ranged in age from five to nine, Belle sold Herman's drugstore and began to run a boarding house. She had no head for business, however, and the venture never prospered. She relied on her children to help her make ends meet.

Pauling recalled that as he grew up, "I had always had small jobs to earn money that helped my mother out at home."[4] The odd jobs Linus found included delivering newspapers, setting pins in a bowling alley, and operating a movie theater projector. Together with two high school friends, Linus also tried his hand at a couple of independent businesses. Linus and his associates built the equipment necessary for their "Palmon Laboratories" to assess the butterfat content of local dairies' products. The dairies, however, were unwilling to give their business to such young entrepreneurs. The photography lab the boys set up in the basement of one of their homes was also short-lived.

Both of these fleeting business ventures were related to chemistry, which is the science of the composition, structure, properties, and reactions of matter. But Linus's first forays into science predated his interest in chemistry. At the age of ninety, Pauling recollected, "When I was eleven years old, with no outside inspiration—just library books—I started collecting insects."[5] In order to kill the specimens he wished to collect, he obtained chemicals from a pharmacist named Ziegler, a former colleague of his father. Elsewhere

BELLE PAULING HOLDS BABY LINUS IN 1901.

Pauling recalled that his interest in insects didn't last very long because "I did not find entomology very satisfying intellectually."[6]

The following year Linus took up another scientifically based collection. Eighty years later Pauling recalled, "When I was twelve years old I began reading about minerals. Agates were about the only minerals that I could collect, but I read books on mineralogy and copied tables of various properties of minerals. I wondered about hardness, streak, color, density, and crystalline face development."[7] Pauling once defined a crystal as "a form of matter in which the component atoms are arranged in a regular, repeating way like bricks in a brick wall."[8] Crystals make up most nonliving substances, including metals, rocks, snowflakes, salt, and sugar. Crystals played an important role in Pauling's later research.

The year after he began collecting minerals, Pauling discovered chemistry. In a long article published in 1970, Pauling remembered, "I became interested in chemistry in 1914, when I was thirteen years old, on the day that a fellow high-school student of my own age (Lloyd A. Jeffress) showed me some chemical experiments in the laboratory that he had set up in the corner of his bedroom. I decided then to be a chemist, and to study chemical engineering, which was, I thought, the profession that chemists followed."[9]

The incident in Jeffress's home lab had such a profound impact on teenaged Linus that he wrote about it often as an adult. When he was 90 he remembered his intellectual response to Jeffress's experiments: "I was really enthralled that you could take a chemical substance and convert it into other substances. Because of that, I became a chemist when I was thirteen years old."[10]

On another occasion Pauling described the practical immediate effect of Jeffress's experiments: "I was intensely interested, and when I reached home I found my father's chemistry book and began reading it, and also carried out a manipulation consisting, I think, only of boiling some water over an alcohol lamp. I immediately began collecting chemicals and apparatus."[11]

Elsewhere Pauling described how he collected what he needed to outfit a home laboratory of his own: "Mr. Ziegler, the druggist who had been my father's friend, now gave me chemicals and some apparatus. Also, a man who lived next door to us, who worked as the stockroom keeper at a dental college, brought home many pieces of glassware for me; they were all chipped and would otherwise have been discarded."[12]

Acquiring everything he wanted to equip his first lab also entailed a little risk-taking. He later recounted, "Almost every weekend I took the train to Oswego, seven miles from Portland, to stay with my [Pauling] grandparents. My grandfather was a night watchman at the foundry there. I would often go down there with him, and then go off to an abandoned smelter about a quarter mile away. It was a wooden structure that was falling down; the laboratory roof had collapsed. But there were hundreds of bottles of chemicals and ore samples. . . . I'd take these things back with me on the train to Portland, then get on the streetcar to travel the two miles to my home."[13]

Linus's discovery of his professional calling did not gladden the hearts of his mother or sisters. His sister

Pauline later reminisced, "He was always experimenting in the basement and the most awful odors would come up and go all through the house. . . . We weren't supposed to go in that little room he closed off down in the basement."[14] His mother was distressed to learn that her son now intended to go to college and even graduate school after completing high school. She wanted him to go to work full time to support the family.

Linus understood the family's economic difficulties, but once he had set his heart on chemistry, he knew what he had to do to be true to himself. He took every course Washington High School offered in science and math. Only one year of chemistry was offered, but the teacher, William V. Greene, provided Linus with opportunities for enrichment. Pauling later recalled, "Frequently, toward the end of the school day, [Greene] would ask me to remain an extra hour to help him in determining the calorific values of the coal and oil the municipal school board purchased. It was probably largely a way of giving me a little extra instruction." In his senior year, Pauling remembered, "Mr. Greene allowed me to work in the chemical laboratory by myself. I used several textbooks, but he would sometimes give me special problems to do. . . . When I got my high school transcript I saw, to my surprise, that he had credited me with an extra year of high school chemistry."[15]

Linus took only one high-school physics course. It introduced him to the laws of matter and energy that underlie chemistry. The physics teacher, Virgil Earle, was also a stickler for correct English usage. He instilled in Pauling a lifelong passion for precision of expression.

Pauling later remembered that his "high school grades

were not outstanding except in the classes that really interested me, such as mathematics and science."[16] But it came as a shock to him to discover that he would be leaving Washington High in spring 1917 without a diploma. Years later he recalled, "I was eager to finish up high school and start college, to prepare myself for a career. To complete the requirements for graduation I needed to take a history course for a year, but in the spring of my senior year they wouldn't let me take the two semesters of the class concurrently. So because I lacked one semester of history, I didn't graduate before going off to OAC [Oregon Agricultural College]."[17] He did not know at the time that in 1962, by which time he had won one Nobel prize and was soon to win a second, Washington High would belatedly award him a diploma.

Luckily, OAC "had no requirements for a high school degree so long as one had enough course credits."[18] But that was not his only reason for choosing to go to college there. He knew they offered a degree in chemical engineering, "which I unquestioningly believed was the right profession for me." More importantly, however, OAC "was the only college I could afford, since we didn't have any money and the tuition was free."[19]

During the summer before he left Portland for Corvallis, where OAC was located, Linus took a job in a machine shop. He impressed his employers so much that they kept raising his salary and encouraged him to continue working rather than leave for college. Since the income was "not insignificant," as Pauling later wrote, his mother also tried to convince him to give up his dreams of college. "I was torn," Pauling remembered, "between my desire to do what my mother wanted me to do and my strong desire to learn more by going to college."[20]

Just as his friendship with Lloyd Jeffress had been instrumental a few years earlier in focusing Linus on a career path, that friendship now kept him from veering from it. Pauling recalled, "By this time Lloyd's father and mother had died and he was living with his aunt and uncle. . . . Lloyd and his aunt and uncle argued with me strongly, urging me not to give up my plan of going to college. My mother accepted this decision, even though the next few years were difficult ones financially for her as well as for me."[21]

During that last summer separating Linus's Oregon boyhood from his college years, he began to keep a diary. Two entries he wrote in September 1917 show how lack of self-confidence gnawed at him on the eve of his departure for OAC. "I will not be able," he worried, "on account of my youth and inexperience, to do justice to the courses and the teaching placed before me." The following day he confided in his diary another concern: "The more I look at myself in the mirror the more peculiar my physiognomy appears to me. I do not look at all attractive."[22]

Before graduating from Oregon Agricultural College, however, Linus Pauling would not only succeed academically but would also prove attractive enough to find the love of his life.

CHAPTER THREE

Undergraduate Years

As he boarded the train for Corvallis on Saturday, October 6, 1917, seventeen-year-old Linus was nervous enough to allow his mother to accompany him. But at the age of ninety he would recall, "when I was in college . . . I began to develop self-confidence, confidence in my own ideas."[1]

Antiwar convictions were not yet among the ideas of the future Nobel peace laureate. The United States was gearing up for World War I. Looking back at that time, Pauling reflected, "Some of the young men who otherwise might have been in college had enlisted, and more would be drafted. Feeling patriotic and wanting to be prepared to fight right away if sent off to war, I signed up for the Student Officers Training Corps—what is ROTC now. I participated in its various training exercises while at OAC, and eventually I achieved the rank of major."[2]

On his arrival at the Corvallis train station, Linus bumped into the head of OAC's math department. In his diary the following day, Linus wrote, "I intend to take every one of the courses offered in Mathematics."[3] He managed to take all the math offered at OAC while he was still a freshman. He later reflected less on the shortcomings of OAC than on his own misconceptions about education: "It did not occur to me at the time that I might have continued learning just by studying mathematics on my own. I thought the only way to learn something was to have some teacher teach you in class."[4]

One of the courses Pauling took his first year introduced him to a field he would later explore in depth: "My first memory about proteins goes back to the spring of 1918, during the First World War, when I was a student in a class on camp cookery . . . as a contribution to the war effort. . . . I remember making a loaf of bread and learning something about the . . . proteins, carbohydrates, and fats." Yet the course did not cover another future passion of his—vitamins—because "it was too soon after the discovery of vitamins for them to get mentioned in the course."[5]

Linus could not devote himself entirely to his studies, however. He had to earn enough money to cover his living expenses. During his first year he worked at menial jobs, "such as chopping wood for the wood stoves and cutting the sides of beef into steaks and roasts." But his instructors soon discovered his intellectual abilities, and by his second year he was supporting himself through academically related work: "the people in the chemical engineering department gave me a job as a stockroom assistant, preparing chemicals for the student laboratories . . . and from then on I at least got enough money to live on and to give some to my mother."[6]

His summer employment followed the same pattern. After his freshman year, he worked in a shipyard on the Oregon coast. After his second year, he spent a month at a job that his mother had found for him. Delivering milk was so boring, however, that he lined up a job with Oregon's highway department working as a paving engineer. He got to use his chemistry background in testing blacktop for the new highway system being laid across the state. He also had time during the evenings, after he retired to the tent that he shared with the crew, to study a chemistry handbook. Since his meals were provided, Linus was able to send his entire salary of $125 a month back home to Belle, who was supposed to safeguard it for his school expenses in the fall.

The end of the summer brought good news and bad. His employers were so pleased with him that they guaranteed him work for as long as he wanted. But when he was about to return to school, Belle told him she had had to use his summer earnings to cover her own expenses. Linus resigned himself to staying on with the highway commission instead of returning to college.

Salvation came unexpectedly. Pauling later recalled, "Somehow the professors in the chemical engineering department heard about my predicament. In the autumn they sent me a telegram offering me a full time position teaching a sophomore class in quantitative chemical analysis. The war was over by then and the university's science classes were being filled by young men released from military service. Though I was still an undergraduate and no older than the students and often even younger than they, I had taken the class . . . and excelled at it. My work in the stockroom, mixing up chemicals for student analysis, had also put me in good stead for this job."[7] Although the salary the department was offering him was $25 less per month than he earned analyzing asphalt, he didn't think twice about that and returned directly to Corvallis.

It was a fateful decision. It not only steered him in the direction of teaching but also introduced him to the field of research that he would himself transform within the decade.

His friend Lloyd Jeffress had predicted a few years earlier that Linus would become a university professor, even though Linus himself continued to say he intended to become a chemical engineer. Now Linus began to focus on his teaching skills. To become a better lecturer, he sought out the professor of oratory, who gave him useful tips. This training would prove useful not only in the classroom but on also every occasion over the years when he spoke publicly on topics ranging from chemical bonds to protein structure to nuclear war to vitamin C.

As Linus's reputation as a fine teacher grew, he earned the nickname "Boy Professor." Soon the chemical engineering department began to assign additional courses to him, sometimes at the request of the students themselves.

The department gave Linus a desk in the departmental library. There he learned touch-typing from the department secretary, whose desk was near his. More important, however, the location of his desk gave him ready access to all the chemistry journals, in which scientists published the results of their research. As Pauling later recalled, "That's how I first developed my interest in the nature of the chemical bond, in 1919. I read the *Journal of the American Chemical Society*. That year there were several papers by Irving Langmuir on the electronic theory of chemical bonding, based upon a paper published in 1916 by Gilbert Newton Lewis."[8]

Before he read these papers, Linus's only concept of how atoms were bound together in molecules or crystals was what he had been taught, and what he proceeded to teach others. As ninety-year-old Pauling would explain, "I used to tell students that the chemical bond could be thought of as a hook and eye. The alkali atoms (sodium and potassium) have an eye, and the halogen elements (chlorine and fluorine, for example) a hook. The chemical bond consisted of the hook hooking into the eye. . . . It really was a primitive picture of chemical bonding, but that was the state of the art. That was the understanding we had of chemical bonds."[9]

Elsewhere Pauling wrote, "It is my memory that I felt reasonably well satisfied with this explanation of chemical bonding—an explanation that seems to me now, with my much greater experience, to be completely unsatisfactory."[10] His eyes were now opened by the papers he read by Lewis and Langmuir. "In 1916 Lewis had proposed that the chemical bond is a pair of electrons held jointly between two nuclei, and during the next three or four years Irving Langmuir developed this idea and applied it in many ways."[11]

These ideas were particularly exciting for Linus to come upon so soon after the discovery of the electron and the nucleus that are the basic parts of every atom in all types of matter. Pauling later conveyed some of this excitement: "Five years before I was born, the existence of the electron was discovered—the negatively charged particle that was making so many modern inventions possible, particularly those using electricity. So I came close to being born in that period of time before it was known that there are electrons in the world! . . . Actually, the nucleus of the atom itself, consisting of the positively charged protons (the number of which balance the number of electrons) plus uncharged neutrons, was not discovered until 1911, when I was ten years old."[12]

No longer content with the hook-and-eye theory himself, Linus did what he could to bring the rest of OAC's chemical engineering department up to date. He presented a seminar to the faculty on the electronic theory of chemical bonding. That year the only other department seminar was about the frozen fish industry, given by a professor of agricultural chemistry. Linus's enthusiasm for the revolutionary idea was more than a flash in the pan. From a vantage point of fifty years later, Pauling described the longterm effect of the Lewis and Langmuir research on him: "It was then. . .that I developed a strong desire to understand the physical and chemical properties of substances in relation to the structure of the atoms and molecules of which they are composed. This desire [which] has largely determined the course of my work. . . . was the result of pure intellectual curiosity."[13]

"I used to tell students that the chemical bond could be thought of as a hook and eye. . . . It really was a primitive picture of chemical bonding."

—Linus Pauling

During his year as an instructor, Linus also broadened his appreciation of world culture by reading widely in other fields. He later said, "in a sense I owed my general education to the library at Oregon Agricultural College. I can remember many of the books that I read. I got from the library in succession, I think, all of the plays that George Bernard Shaw had written. I can remember reading Voltaire's poems . . . and there were many other books."[14]

In the end, the 1919–20 academic year turned out to be a blessing in disguise instead of an unwelcome disruption in Linus's undergraduate career. Linus was now confident enough to joke around with his teachers, sometimes at their expense. A fellow chemical engineering student, Paul Emmett, would later marry Pauling's sister, Pauline. Emmett remembered this incident: "our new physical chemistry teacher, in correcting problems, said, 'Well, now, since Linus Pauling and I get the same answer, when two great authorities agree, it must be right.' Linus calmly looked him in the eye and said, 'Who's the other one?'"[15]

Linus had turned into much more than a smug joker, however. He was also confident enough now to believe in his own ability to become a serious and productive scientist. He later recalled his realization "that I myself might discover something new about the nature of the world, and also have some new ideas that contributed to a better understanding of the universe."[16]

When Linus returned to Corvallis as a full-time student in fall 1920, there were few courses for him to take. He had thought about transferring to the California Institute of Technology. During his sophomore year he had learned about the institute from the chairman of the chemical engineering department at OAC, John Fulton. Fulton had shown him an advertisement from Caltech describing fellowships in chemistry offered to graduate students and suggested it might be a good place for Linus to study some day. Linus wrote a letter inquiring about the feasibility of transferring. The response, however, indicated that the Caltech course load was so heavy that he would not be able to work on the side to earn his living expenses. So transferring was out of the question.

The department at OAC knew what an asset he was, however. They gave him opportunities to compensate for the skimpy course offerings by doing additional teaching and assisting. In his last semester before graduating in 1922, Linus was happy to earn some extra cash by teaching a section of freshman chemistry to home economics majors. It was another fateful decision.

When he first arrived at OAC in fall 1917, Linus developed a crush on a girl named Irene Sparks. But either his dating skills or his ability to pay for dates or both must have been inadequate. As a sophomore he became a member of the Gamma Tau Beta fraternity. According to its rules, every new fraternity brother had to have a date each weekend. Whoever failed in this respect was punished by being submerged in a cold bath. When Linus failed to live up to the dating requirement, he came up with a plan. While he was being carried to the bathtub, he breathed deeply, knowing he could in this way saturate his blood with oxygen. He later remembered, "I didn't struggle at all. . . . They put me in the tub, holding me under the water, and I just lay there . . . and the seconds went by . . . a minute went by . . . and they pulled me out, very frightened, saying, 'He's had a heart attack or something!' Of course, I 'recovered,' and from then on didn't have to worry about it."[17]

Now in the spring of his senior year all twenty-five students in his freshman chemistry for home economics class were female. On the first day he called on one whose name he knew he would not embarrass himself by mispronouncing: Ava Helen Miller. She not only answered his question well—"to explain the chemical action of the ingredients in baking powder"—but also captured his heart.[18] As graduation drew near, he had to let her know his feelings for her without overstepping the boundaries that kept instructors from dating their students.

On one assignment he returned to her, he wrote, "You are to understand that an instructor has been very much criticized for the attention he paid one of his students. I hope this does not happen to me."[19] Although she was annoyed by the implication that she was flirting with him, she accepted an invitation to join him on a walk across campus. Within a short time they were engaged. In order to avoid the accusation of showing her any favoritism, he gave her a lower mark for the course than she actually deserved.

Ava Helen, like Linus, had been raised by a single mother, but the similarity in their upbringings did not go much beyond that. While Belle Pauling had no interest in politics or ideas, Ava Helen's mother had been involved in the struggle to secure for women the right to vote. While Belle Pauling resented her son's determination to get an education beyond high school, Ava Helen's mother struggled to put as many of her twelve children as possible through college. Nonetheless, both mothers agreed that the couple was too young to marry.

Linus followed his mother's advice about postponing the marriage, but he would listen to her only up to a certain point. As Pauling later told it, "By my junior year I was already thinking about going to graduate school. . . . As before, my mother did not appreciate my desire to continue

LINUS PAULING'S GRADUATION PORTRAIT FROM OREGON AGRICULTURAL
COLLEGE, CIRCA MAY 1922.

on with my schooling and not get a well-paid regular job in some industry, as she expected me to do after five years at OAC."[20]

In addition to applying to Caltech, Pauling also sent in applications to Berkeley, where his hero Gilbert N. Lewis was dean of the college of chemistry, and to Harvard. He heard first from Harvard, which offered him a half-time instructorship. He turned down the offer, however, when he learned it would take six years to complete his doctorate. He next heard from Arthur A. Noyes, head of the division of chemistry and chemical engineering at Caltech. Noyes offered him a part-time appointment as an instructor and researcher and indicated that he might expect to complete his degree in three years. Since Noyes demanded an immediate response to the offer, Linus accepted without having heard from Berkeley.

Noyes then wrote back suggesting some ways in which Linus could use his summer to prepare for the rigorous work that would be expected of him at Caltech. He sent Linus the proofs of a new edition of his textbook, *Chemical Principles*, and assigned him the task of figuring out all the problems in the first nine chapters. As Pauling later recalled, "This book was an excellent one for independent study. I worked the problems without any trouble during the evenings of the summer of 1922."[21]

Having learned from Linus about his longtime interest in minerals and crystals, Noyes also suggested that Linus do doctoral research on the structure of crystals. In order to prepare himself for such work, Noyes suggested that Linus read *X-Rays and Crystal Structure*. Linus went to great lengths to find the book, by British physicists W. H. Bragg and W. L. Bragg, who had figured out a technique that used X-rays to uncover crystal structure. After reading the book, Linus wrote Noyes that he would be happy to do doctoral research in that field.

Linus's career as an undergraduate was now at an end. The nervous boy who had arrived in Corvallis nearly five years earlier was now the man chosen to deliver the senior class oration at commencement. Linus concluded his speech by encouraging his classmates to show their gratitude to OAC through "service to our fellow men."[22] Just how he would follow his own advice, however, could not yet be predicted.

CHAPTER FOUR

PASADENA AND EUROPE

In 1965 Pauling wrote, "I now have the opinion that I had the greatest good luck in having gone to Pasadena in 1922. I do not think that I could have found better conditions for preparation for a career in physical chemistry anywhere else in the world."[1] In 1922 Pauling was a new graduate student, but Caltech itself was still a young institution. Once known as Throop Polytechnic Institute, it had recently taken a new name and a new mission. Instead of a local vocational school, it would strive to become a major scientific research center. Only the year before Pauling's arrival had the best known physicist in the U.S., Robert A. Millikan, come to Pasadena to head the transformation. A few years earlier, in 1917, Arthur A. Noyes had been brought out west from the Massachusetts Institute of Technology (MIT) to run the chemistry division. When Pauling arrived, Caltech had a faculty of eighteen, with twenty-nine graduate students, ten of whom were working toward doctorates in chemistry. No one knew at the time that Pauling would be associated with Caltech for forty-one years. During that time he would turn it into an international center of chemistry research.

Pauling later remembered the important role several professors at Caltech played in shaping his career. Although Pauling took only one course from Noyes, the latter played the major role in determining the overall pattern of Pauling's career. Before Pauling's arrival, Noyes had decided to make Caltech the first U.S. institution to use the new technique of X-ray crystallography to do chemistry research. X-ray crystallography uses X-ray diffraction to study the structure of crystals. When X-rays are directed through the atoms of a crystal, the atoms scatter the X-rays. The result is a pattern that reveals information about the three-dimensional arrangement of atoms in the crystal. Noyes believed that structure was the key to chemical behavior. For example, he believed the reason some types of matter combine easily while others do not could be traced to differences in their atomic structure. Now that X-ray crystallography allowed scientists to understand the three-dimensional structure of matter at the atomic level, Noyes was determined to put it to use at Caltech.

Pauling later said that two other Caltech professors "were probably most important in the early period of my career."[2] One of these was his thesis advisor, Roscoe Gilkey Dickinson. Dickinson had been an undergraduate at MIT. When Noyes moved to Caltech from MIT, Dickinson followed him. In 1920 Dickinson became the first person to earn a doctorate in chemistry at Caltech.

Pauling later reflected on what he had learned from Dickinson. Thanks to Dickinson, he mastered the X-ray diffraction method. Pauling later recalled: "I was very excited about it, and it only took him a couple of months to teach me how to determine the structure of a rather simple crystal by taking X-ray diffraction photographs of it and analyzing those photographs."[3] Elsewhere Pauling wrote, "I consider my entry into the field of X-ray crystallography, nine years after it had been developed, to be just about the most fortunate accident that I have experienced in my life. . . . It was clear that much additional information about the nature of the chemical bond was being provided and was going to be provided in the future by the determination of the structure of crystals by the X-ray diffraction method."[4]

But Dickinson taught Pauling something even more valuable than a specific research method: "how to assess the reliability of my own conclusions. He taught me to ask every time I reached some conclusion: 'Have I made some assumption in reaching this conclusion? And what is the assumption? And what are the chances that this assumption is wrong? How reliable is the conclusion?'" According to Pauling, "I have remembered this ever since and have continued to feel grateful to him."[5]

Noyes's course was the only chemistry course Pauling took in graduate school. In order to deepen his understanding of the mechanical and electrical forces that underlie chemical properties, Pauling concentrated on math and physics courses. The second Caltech professor to play a crucial role in Pauling's early career was a professor of physical chemistry and mathematical physics, Richard Chace Tolman. Tolman arrived at Caltech only a year before Pauling. He was among a handful of American scientists at the time who grasped the crucial importance of the quantum theory being developed in Europe. Quantum theory was a new way to use mathematics to understand how matter worked at the atomic level. Because it called into question many ideas about physics that scientists had taken as facts for centuries, quantum theory was resisted by many scientists for some time.

Pauling took all of Tolman's courses on quantum theory. Within a few years, Pauling would use quantum mechanics (a later form of quantum theory) to explain chemical structure. This achievement is considered one of the most important advances in twentieth-century science.

Pauling never forgot an important lesson he learned as a result of an interaction with Tolman. "One episode," he recalled, "impressed itself on my memory so strongly that I conclude it had a significant impact on my development. In the spring of 1923 Tolman asked me a question during a seminar. My answer was 'I don't know; I haven't taken a course in that subject.' At the end of the seminar [a postdoctoral fellow] took me to one side and said, 'Linus, you shouldn't have answered Professor Tolman the way you did; you are a graduate student now, and you are supposed to know everything.'"[6]

Also important in Pauling's development were European physicists participating in the quantum revolution who lectured at Caltech during his first years there. Of these, the most important was Arnold Sommerfeld, director of the Institute of Theoretical Physics in Munich. Sommerfeld was a close colleague of Niels Bohr, the great Danish physicist, who in 1913 had first used quantum theory to explain the structure of the atom.

In his first year at Caltech, Pauling heard Sommerfeld

lecture on the quantum model of the atom. After class one day Pauling showed Sommerfeld some wire-and-wood models he had made. Pauling had designed the models to show how the placement of electrons in the Bohr-Sommerfeld atom could explain how carbon formed chemical bonds. Pauling's 3-D model turned out to be wrong. Making such models, however, would later enable Pauling to reach many correct conclusions (and also some other incorrect ones).

By being at Caltech at just this time, Pauling was trained to do pathbreaking work both as an experimentalist and as a theoretician. By carrying out carefully designed experiments, experimentalists collect data that can demonstrate how substances behave. They compare their results to the theories developed by theoreticians to explain why nature works as it does. The goal is to make theories fit experimental findings. Near the end of his life Pauling wrote, "I was fortunate to be able to participate not only in the experimental field of X-ray crystallography but also in the theoretical field of quantum mechanics, especially in its application to the question of the nature of the chemical bond."[7]

In June 1925 Caltech awarded Pauling a doctorate with highest honors in chemistry, with minors in physics and mathematics. His doctoral thesis, "The Determination with X-rays of the Structure of Crystals," was based on five papers he had previously published. He also had another seven published papers to his credit.

Pauling's life at Caltech changed dramatically after his first year. In 1922–23 Pauling lived with his OAC friend (and future brother-in-law) Paul Emmett and Emmett's mother in Pasadena. The two new graduate students had an unusual sleeping schedule. Emmett slept in their shared bed until 3:00 A.M., while Pauling worked in the lab. When Pauling went to bed, Emmett got up to begin his day's studying.

Although Pauling and Ava Helen exchanged daily letters, they missed each other too much to remain separated. Despite family opposition, the young couple married on June 17, 1923. After a brief honeymoon, Pauling began his last summer as a pavement analyst for the Oregon highway department. Instead of living in the tent with the crew, the newlyweds rented rooms as the crew traveled through the state laying roads.

Pauling had already seen some evidence that Ava Helen sometimes knew more than he did. In one of his daily letters he happened to misidentify the type of acid present in sauerkraut. As he later recounted, "I got back a letter saying '—any damned fool knows that . . . it's lactic acid [in sauerkraut]!'"[8] During the summer of 1923 he discovered more about her intelligence. They often whiled away the evening hours taking intelligence tests they found in a book Pauling borrowed from a local library. Often Ava Helen beat Pauling in speedily and accurately working out the math problems. He would later recall humorously that those tests "showed that my wife was smarter than I. Since we were already married, it was too late for me to do anything about it."[9]

In fall 1923 the Paulings moved into a small apartment near Caltech. Until the birth in March 1925 of the first of their four children, Ava Helen helped Pauling in the lab, in constructing 3-D models of crystals, and in making measurements and calculations.

Lloyd Jeffress, Pauling's best friend from high school, had been the best man at the Paulings' wedding. While Pauling was doing his graduate work at Caltech, Jeffress was working toward his doctorate in psychology at Berkeley. During a visit to Jeffress, Pauling introduced himself to G. N. Lewis, whose paper on the role of electrons in chemical bonding had so impressed him in 1919–20. After Pauling told Lewis of his work on crystals at Caltech, Lewis said he would gladly consider taking Pauling on as a postdoctoral fellow at Berkeley after he finished his Ph.D.

When Noyes learned of Lewis's interest in Pauling, he began to scheme to keep Pauling at Caltech. Noyes had singled out Pauling as a rising star by the time Pauling had completed his first semester at Caltech. In February 1923 Noyes wrote an old friend, "One of our Fellows, who came from Oregon, is also proving quite exceptional."[10] Noyes had taken a risk in admitting Pauling to Caltech from OAC. OAC, after all, had no chemistry major and no research program. It not only offered no advanced courses in physical chemistry but even its introductory course was based on an inadequate textbook. But now, as Pauling approached the completion of his Ph.D., Noyes knew how well his risk had paid off. He identified Pauling as "the ablest candidate for the doctor's degree in chemistry who has yet attended this Institute."[11]

Now that Pauling had graduated with distinction, what would he do next? He later wrote, "When I was approaching the completion of my work for the Ph.D. there were many National Research Council fellows in Pasadena, and I applied for a National Research Council fellowship, saying in my application that I would go to Berkeley and work with Gilbert Newton Lewis."[12] To keep Pauling from going to Berkeley after he was awarded the NRC fellowship, Noyes told him, "You have done a large amount of X-ray work that you haven't yet written up for publication. That work could most conveniently be done here in Pasadena, so why don't you just stay here and complete writing the papers?"[13]

So Pauling spent the first months of his NRC fellowship finishing up work he had begun at Caltech. Just when Pauling was thinking of moving to Berkeley, as he had promised the NRC, Noyes suggested he apply for a new fellowship just established by the Guggenheim family foundation. Noyes told Pauling he would benefit from studying the new developments in quantum theory being worked out by physicists in Europe. G. N. Lewis agreed that such a trip would be beneficial.

> *"[Pauling is] the ablest candidate for the doctor's degree in chemistry who has yet attended [Caltech]."*
>
> **—Arthur A. Noyes**

In December 1925 Pauling applied for a Guggenheim. He proposed "to apply quantum mechanics, discovered only a few months earlier, to the problem of the structure of molecules and the nature of the chemical bond."[14] Encouraged by Noyes to believe that he would be awarded the fellowship, Pauling wrote to Niels Bohr in Copenhagen and Arnold Sommerfeld in Munich to see if either would welcome him as a postdoctoral fellow at his institute of theoretical physics.

Lest Pauling be tempted to go to Berkeley in the few

months before he left for Europe, Noyes made him an offer he could not resist. Noyes invited Linus, Ava Helen, and their nine-month-old son, Linus Jr., to dinner on Christmas 1925. He recommended that the Paulings go to Europe as tourists before the Guggenheim fellowship came through. He offered them money to cover not only their fare but also their living expenses until the fellowship money became available.

On his twenty-fifth birthday, February 28, 1926, Pauling resigned his NRC fellowship. The NRC wrote him a letter chastising him for having broken his promise to go to Berkeley. Soon thereafter the Paulings set sail for Europe. At Ava Helen's suggestion, the couple left their infant son with her mother, whom they paid $25 a month to raise their son. Although they kept track of the baby's development by exchanging letters, they did not see their firstborn for over a year and a half.

Since Pauling never heard back from Bohr, they traveled to Munich, where they arrived in late April 1926. Shortly thereafter Pauling received official notice that he had been awarded a Guggenheim fellowship. He was one of thirty-five fellows that year.

While the Paulings were sailing to Europe, physicist Erwin Schrödinger published a new mathematical approach to quantum theory. At first glance Schrödinger's so-called wave mechanics seemed to conflict with the system developed in summer 1925 by Bohr's protégé, Werner Heisenberg. Later in 1926, however, a number of physicists determined that these two new mathematical approaches could be used interchangeably. Each one improved upon Bohr's quantum theory.

During his time in Munich Pauling never went to the university's Institute of Physical Chemistry. All his interactions were with theoretical physicists. Pauling was the only chemist at Sommerfeld's institute. He had the insight to see that the new quantum physics would explain molecular structure, which in turn would explain why matter behaved the way it did.

In summer 1926, having met not only with Sommerfeld but also with other, younger scientists who were revolutionizing quantum theory, Pauling wrote Noyes that he was "now working on the new quantum mechanics" that expanded and refined Bohr's work, "for I think that atomic and molecular chemistry will require it."[15]

During the same summer Pauling received sad news from home. His mother's pernicious anemia had worsened after a bout of flu. Belle then contracted pneumonia and began to have delusions. She was hospitalized in an institution in Salem, Oregon, that treated mainly the insane. She died there at the age of forty-five. In those days, travel to Europe was possible only by ship, and Pauling was unable to return for the funeral.

That autumn Pauling took Sommerfeld's first course on wave mechanics. By early 1927 Pauling had published two papers that applied the new quantum mechanical techniques to the study of both atoms and crystals. He used his skills in X-ray crystallography to test the results of his wave mechanical calculations. He also used his wave mechanical calculations to check the results of his X-ray crystallographic data. Pauling began to develop a set of general rules based on quantum mechanics that explained crystal structure. His international reputation began to grow.

Pauling felt he needed more time in Europe to gain a better understanding of the nature of the chemical bond that kept matter together. He applied for and was granted a six-month extension of his Guggenheim fellowship. Sommerfeld supported his application with a strong letter of recommendation. "My colleagues and I have the impression that he is an extraordinary, productive scientist with many interests, in whom it is justified to place the greatest expectations."[16]

During his extended fellowship, Pauling traveled from Munich to Copenhagen, Göttingen, and Zurich, all centers of the quantum revolution. He arrived at Bohr's Institute of Theoretical Physics in Copenhagen without a formal invitation. Bohr was too busy to pay much attention to him, and he had only one brief interview with the great man. Pauling had trouble understanding Bohr, and later said, "Bohr usually spoke in a mixture of English and other languages, and he was very hard to understand because he didn't pronounce the words easily."[17] But he did useful work with one of Bohr's younger colleagues, Samuel Goudsmit. In 1930 a book Pauling coauthored with Goudsmit, *The Structure of Line Spectra*, was published in the United States.

In Göttingen Pauling met an American graduate student in physics, J. Robert Oppenheimer. Years later, as head of the American program to build the atomic bomb during World War II, Oppenheimer tried unsuccessfully to recruit Pauling.

In Zurich Pauling discovered that two German friends from Munich, philosopher Walter Heitler and physicist Fritz London, had discovered a way to use some of the new quantum mechanical techniques to explain the way two hydrogen atoms bonded together to form a stable hydrogen molecule. Although Pauling admired their work, he believed it was much too mathematically complicated to be useful to most chemists. He later described his reaction to the Heitler-London publication: "I thought there was a possibility of doing something better but I didn't know what it was that needed to be done. Here I think I had the feeling that if I worked in the field I probably would find something, make some discovery, and that the probability was high enough to justify my working in the field."[18]

Pauling spent much of the rest of his time in Europe and en route home in early September 1927 thinking about how he could both extend and simplify the ideas of Heitler and London so that chemists would understand them. He would also spend the next decade of his life working in this field. By using quantum mechanics he would explain the bonds that hold matter together. He would show how the nature of these bonds, in turn, explain why different types of molecules have different properties. He would show how the distances and angles between the atoms that make up molecules determine why some substances, for example, react with water and air while others do not.

Years later, Pauling reflected on his nineteen months in Europe in 1926 and 1927. "I was very fortunate to have gone to Sommerfeld's Institute of Theoretical Physics just at that time. For many years much of my work has consisted of the application of quantum mechanics to chemical problems. . . . My year in Munich was very productive. . . . I was able to begin attacking many problems dealing with the nature of the chemical bond by applying quantum mechanics to these problems."[19]

In late spring 1927, Noyes wrote Pauling, offering him a position at Caltech. Pauling accepted the offer to return to Caltech that fall as an assistant professor of theoretical chemistry and mathematical physics.

It took Pauling many years to figure out just how Noyes had manipulated things. "It wasn't until about twenty years later," he later wrote, "that I realized that Noyes was afraid that I would become a member of the staff at Berkeley if I took up my fellowship in Berkeley." He also learned the purpose of a visit that G. N. Lewis had paid to Pasadena around the time Pauling received his Ph.D. "Many years later I learned that he had come to offer me an appointment, but that Noyes had talked him out of it."

But Pauling forgave Noyes. "I think that it was probably a good thing that Noyes carried out his machinations. It was a fine experience for me to work in the young and growing institution, the California Institute of Technology."[20]

CHAPTER FIVE

BRIDGING CHEMISTRY AND PHYSICS

Pauling's unique training enabled him to work on the frontiers of science. He made many discoveries along the borders where different sciences meet. His work straddled the borders between chemistry and physics, chemistry and biology, and chemistry and medicine.

In December 1926, while still in Europe, Pauling wrote Noyes, "Some people seem to think that work such as mine, dealing with the properties of atoms and molecules, should be classed with physics but I . . . feel that the study of chemical substances remains chemistry."[1] Many years later he wrote, "Usually, I say I am a chemist; sometimes I say I am a physical chemist. Probably I should say I am a physicist with an interest in chemistry."[2]

Pauling understood that straddling borders gave him an edge on other scientists. Toward the end of his life he reflected: "I recognize that many physicists are smarter than I am—most of them theoretical physicists. . . . I console myself with the thought that although they may be smarter and may be deeper thinkers than I am, I have broader interests than they have. I don't suppose anybody else in the world has a good background, knowledge of physics, mathematics, theoretical physics, *and* knows a great deal about chemistry—the amount that I know."[3]

When Pauling returned to Pasadena in fall 1927, he understood that only a handful of American chemists knew enough quantum mechanics to bring chemistry into line with it. The field lay wide open for someone with his preparation and abilities. He had been told by Noyes that he was returning to an appointment as assistant professor not only of theoretical chemistry but also of mathematical physics. He discovered upon returning to Caltech, however, that the second title had been dropped. Pauling later decided that Noyes didn't want his star chemist straying too far into physics. It was possible, he thought, that Noyes "may have decided that he didn't want me to be associated with the physics department . . . that perhaps I would shift."[4]

Pauling soon began using his exceptionally broad training to make his mark. In 1928 he reported that quantum mechanics could explain why the carbon atom—with its six electrons—formed the kinds of bonds it did with other atoms. It took nearly three years, however, to reduce his complicated equations to a form that "would be convincing to anybody."[5]

In the fall of 1930, he began to make use of the work of physicist John Slater, who had simplified Schrödinger's equation in a way that seemed useful to Pauling. One night in December of that year, Pauling discovered a shortcut that enabled him to make his own necessary mathematical simplifications. He recalled the moment as one of the most professionally exciting times in his life: "I was so excited and happy. I think I stayed up all night, making, writing out, solving the equations, which were so simple that I could solve them in a few minutes. . . . I just kept getting more and more euphorious as time went by."[6]

After two more months of work, Pauling summed up his research in a landmark paper that laid out six rules, based on quantum mechanics, that explained how shared electrons formed bonds. This paper, among the most important in the history of chemistry, was published in 1931. He called it "The Nature of the Chemical Bond." It was the first of seven papers (and, later, a landmark book) he would publish under that title.

> *"Usually, I say I am a chemist; sometimes I say I am a physical chemist. Probably I should say I am a physicist with an interest in chemistry."*
>
> **—Linus Pauling**

Nearly sixty years later Pauling said, "I considered that paper . . . as my most important paper, and I believe I am right in saying that is the one that developed the greatest feeling of excitement in me."[7] Elsewhere Pauling called that paper "the most important part of the work for which I was awarded the Nobel Prize in Chemistry in 1954."[8] Building on the work of London, Heitler, and Slater, Pauling succeeded in this series of papers in demonstrating how quantum mechanics made sense of the molecules with which chemists work. That achievement is now considered one of the most important accomplishments of twentieth-century science.

At the same time he was doing groundbreaking work on the nature of the chemical bond, Pauling continued X-ray crystallography work on the structure of crystals. Now head of Caltech's X-ray laboratory, he was determined to use the technique to find the rules that governed the structure of crystals. Success would enable him to predict how unknown crystals were put together.

English crystallographer William Lawrence Bragg, working in his laboratory in Manchester, England, had set himself the same task. Bragg was coauthor, with his father, of the book on X-ray crystallography that Noyes had suggested Pauling read in the summer of 1922. Now Pauling, a relative newcomer, was poised to give the older scientist a run for his money. It would not be the only time that Pauling and Bragg would set their eyes on the same scientific prize.

Both Pauling and Bragg focused on silicates—crystals that combine atoms of silicon, oxygen, and different metals. Some silicates are very common minerals, but their structures are complicated. Pauling devised 3-D models of these structures. He drew possible structures on paper, which he then folded, and, with Ava Helen's help, sewed together. In 1928 he published a set of rules that governed the structures of ionic crystals. These came to be called "Pauling's rules."

Bragg was disappointed that it was Pauling rather than he who authored the rules. Nonetheless, he conceded their importance to chemistry. In 1937, for example, Bragg graciously said that Pauling's rules were "the basis for

LINUS PAULING STANDS BEFORE ONE OF HIS FAMOUS 3-D MOLECULAR MODELS.

stereochemistry of minerals."[9] (Stereochemistry deals with the spatial arrangements of atoms in substances and how these arrangements affect their properties.)

Using his rules, Pauling was able to solve the structure of several silicates and thereby explain their properties. The crystal structures he uncovered explained, for example, why mica splits into thin, flexible, transparent sheets, while talc—the softest mineral—splits so completely on the microscopic scale that it simply crumbles on the macroscopic scale. Many years later Pauling told a radio interviewer what pleasure he had taken in discovering the structure of a particular crystal sixty years earlier. "I was feeling happy because I had in my pocket a crystal of sulvanite. . . . And . . . I had just determined the structure . . . of this and it was a very striking structure . . . it didn't fit in with my ideas about sulfide minerals. But I knew what the structure was, nobody else knows, nobody in the world knows what the structure is and they won't know until I tell them. This is an example of the feeling of pleasure I had on discovering something new in the world."[10]

Pauling's success in using both quantum mechanics and X-ray diffraction to solve basic problems in crystal structure and physical chemistry led to several job offers. He turned down an offer from Harvard but used it to extract from Caltech a promotion, a pay raise, travel money, more lab support, and a month's leave each year. The leave would finally enable Pauling to realize his dream of working with G. N. Lewis at the University of California at Berkeley.

In spring 1930 the Paulings (this time with five-year-old Linus in tow) again traveled to Europe. Their first stop was Manchester, where he met Bragg for the first time.

Bragg was polite and helpful personally but not profession-ally. He did not invite Pauling to give a talk, for example. That summer Pauling returned to Sommerfeld's Institute for Theoretical Physics in Munich. There he continued to work on quantum mechanics. A visit to a Viennese colleague, Hermann Mark, who worked in nearby Ludwigshafen, proved especially beneficial. Mark introduced Pauling to the technique of electron-diffraction photography, which he had not encountered before. The equipment enabled researchers to study the structure of individual molecules. While the photographs for X-ray diffraction could some-times require hours, electron diffraction required only a fraction of a second. As a result, the technique could be used to study many more substances than X-ray diffraction could.

Mark had recently used the electron-diffraction tech-nique to determine the structure of gas molecules of benzene and carbon tetrachloride. He told Pauling that he had no further plans to use the technique himself. He was happy to have Pauling make use of the technique in his own lab at Caltech. Mark gave Pauling plans for building an identical machine at Caltech. One of Pauling's graduate stu-dents constructed such an apparatus. Pauling and his coworkers then used it to work out the structures of approximately 225 molecules over the next quarter-century.

By the time Pauling turned thirty in 1931, he was the author of more than fifty papers on topics both theoretical and experimental. Most were on the chemical bond or mol-ecular structure. That year Pauling became the first recipient of the American Chemical Society's annual prize to the best young American chemist. *Scientific American* called him "a prodigy of American science." The magazine reported that the donor of the prize considered Pauling "a rising star, who may yet win the Nobel Prize."[11]

As job offers continued to come Pauling's way, Caltech promoted him to full professor of chemistry, continued to raise his salary, and lightened his teaching responsibilities so he could devote most of his time to research. In May 1933 he became at thirty-two one of the youngest people ever elected to the extremely prestigious National Academy of Sciences.[12]

Although Pauling had a reduced teaching load, he nonetheless believed that preparing the chemists of the future was an important calling. He devised an exciting introductory course that made use of his ideas about the chemical bond to explain the structure of molecules and to demonstrate how structure was responsible for chemical reactions and properties. According to biophysicist Alexander Rich, "Pauling [was] a stimulating and lively lecturer; for many years he taught the first-year general chemistry course at Caltech. He greatly enjoyed direct contact with freshmen."[13]

Pauling was an inspiring teacher, and a very informal one. Crystallographer David Shoemaker remembered that Pauling was sometimes quite physically active while he lectured. "Some have called it . . . 'classroom calisthenics'—leaps from the classroom floor to a sitting position on the lecture desk with legs dangling, or parallel bar exercises with one hand on the chalk tray and the other on the lecture podium, the body swinging back and forth while the lecture was going on at the same time."[14]

Pauling often used visual aids in class to demonstrate his

points. Chemist Dudley Herschbach remembered going into Pauling's office for the first time and encountering "a profuse collection of molecular models some with atoms nearly the size of basketballs and bonds like baseball bats."[15]

In June 1936 Pauling's mentor Arthur Noyes died after a battle with cancer. In 1927 Noyes had called Pauling his "understudy."[16] Some years later, Noyes said of Pauling, "Were all the rest of the Chemistry Dept. wiped away except P., it would still be one of the most important departments of chemistry in the world."[17] Despite the objections of some of the older faculty, in 1937 Caltech appointed thirty-six-year-old Pauling chair of Caltech's Division of Chemistry and Chemical Engineering and director of the institute's chemical laboratories.

Pauling proved an able chairman and research director. Although Caltech had many more students than it had when he arrived fifteen years earlier, he succeeded in maintaining the close relationship between students and faculty that had meant so much to him then. Pauling never forgot how important it was for him as a graduate student to have informal opportunities "to come into close contact with members of the faculty," because such "occasions gave opportunity for the unhurried discussion of scientific and practical problems."[18] Now, as director of graduate and undergraduate students himself, he often hosted informal gatherings of students and postdoctoral fellows at his home. Just as Noyes had taken twenty-one-year-old Pauling on camping trips, Pauling now took his own students on such outings.

In the fall of 1937, the newly promoted Pauling spent the semester at Cornell University with Ava Helen. They left their three-month-old son, five-year-old daughter, and two older sons of twelve and six with Pauling's secretary in Pasadena. As Cornell's George Fisher Baker Lecturer, Pauling was expected to give a series of lectures on a unified theme. The lectures would then be edited into a book. The result was *The Nature of the Chemical Bond and the Structure of Molecules and Crystals: An Introduction to Modern Structural Chemistry*. Published in 1939, the book stayed in print for nearly thirty years. It became one of the most influential books in the history of chemistry.

Aimed at graduate students in chemistry, *The Nature of the Chemical Bond* was used at most of the top American universities. Many other readers made use of the book, not only in English, but also in its French, Japanese, German, Russian, and Spanish editions. Its language was straightforward, its drawings and diagrams were appealing and instructive, and it included just enough math. The book went to great lengths to set aside chemists' fears that quantum mechanics was beyond their understanding. In the introduction to the book, Pauling wrote, "I formed the opinion that, even though much of the recent progress in structural chemistry has been due to quantum mechanics, it should be possible to describe the new developments in a thorough-going and satisfactory manner without the use of advanced mathematics."[19]

The Nature of the Chemical Bond introduced its readers to Pauling's ideas about the chemical bond, which were grounded in the principles of quantum mechanics. The book also stressed the importance of X-ray diffraction and electron-diffraction techniques for determining the length of the bonds between atoms and the angles between bonds.

Pauling dedicated the book to G. N. Lewis. On August 25, 1939, Lewis wrote Pauling: "I have returned from a short vacation for which the only books I took were half a dozen detective stories and your 'Chemical Bond.' I found yours the most exciting of the lot. I cannot tell you how much I appreciate having a book dedicated to me which is such a very important contribution."[20]

Pauling went on to write other influential chemistry books. His introductory college textbook, *General Chemistry*, was published in 1947. Without actually treating quantum mechanics as such, the text was the first to incorporate quantum mechanical principles. It was also the first organized around the themes of chemical bonding and molecular structure. The well-illustrated book was widely adopted and translated into thirteen languages. Earlier introductory textbooks had often seemed a collection of facts to be memorized. According to Alexander Rich, *General Chemistry* "revolutionized the teaching of the subject because it presented chemistry as a subject to be understood rationally in terms of molecular structure and the laws of atomic physics."[21]

In 1950 Pauling's *College Chemistry*—a simpler version of *General Chemistry*—was published. It, too, was a major success. Royalties from the textbooks enabled the Paulings to construct a swimming pool on the grounds of their unusual home. Situated about five miles from the Caltech campus, the house was built in the late 1930s. Pauling had asked the architect to design it with two long wings joined at an angle. He hoped for a precise 109.4667-degree angle, to mimic the most common angle between bonds in carbon in living systems and in diamonds. The architect, however, convinced Pauling to settle for an angle that was less difficult to execute. With an angle of 120 degrees joining its wings, the house's structure mimicked the bond angle in benzene.

Pauling felt that by 1935 he had "an essentially complete understanding of the nature of the chemical bond. . . . developed in large part through the direct application of quantum mechanical principles to the problem of the electronic structure of molecules."[22] Pauling's research interests shortly thereafter broadened into other areas. Nonetheless, he continued to work both on chemical bonding and structural chemistry over the next decades. In the early 1950s, for example, he published important work on phosphorus bonding. He also showed how water molecules could form hydrogen-bonded, ice-like crystals containing microscopic "cages" that could entrap gas molecules.

Pauling's research along the boundaries between chemistry and physics succeeded in solving some basic problems. His work on the nature of the chemical bond shed new light on how atoms combined to form a stable molecule. It also explained why atoms join together to produce certain stable substances but not others. These explanations helped earn him the Nobel Prize in chemistry in 1954.

CHAPTER SIX

BRIDGING CHEMISTRY, BIOLOGY, AND MEDICINE

Pauling's tendency to work on the borders between scientific disciplines helped inaugurate a new scientific field. Molecular biology is the study of the molecules that govern molecular processes in living organisms. The term was first used in 1938 in reference to "those borderline areas in which physics and chemistry merge with biology."[1] In 1935 Pauling began serious work bridging chemistry and biology, and he is considered one of the fathers of the field. Today's genetic engineering and other forms of biotechnology make use of the results of molecular biological research.

How did Pauling make the leap from crystallography and structural chemistry to biochemistry—the chemistry of biological substances and biological processes? The need to find funding for his growing research laboratories during the Depression changed the course of his career. The Depression was the serious worldwide economic slump that began in the late 1920s and ended only with World War II in the 1940s. During the Depression, Caltech ran into financial difficulties. Institutional support for research dried up. The Rockefeller Foundation was eager to support work like Pauling's—but only if he would apply his knowledge of math, physics, and chemistry to biology.

Pauling had never had a formal course in biology. He lacked a strong background even in organic chemistry—the study of the molecules based on carbon that are the basis of all living things. Nonetheless, Pauling understood that to secure support from the Rockefeller Foundation he would have to become "interested in chemistry in relation to biology."[2] So Pauling began to work with his usual energy and excitement on the structure of biological molecules. He focused on proteins, complex molecules that are necessary for the chemical processes that occur in living organisms. Proteins exist in every cell and are essential to plant and animal life. Scientists in the 1930s had no idea what proteins looked like or how they functioned. They believed, however, that revealing the structure of proteins might shed light on many unanswered questions.

Aware of gaps in his knowledge, Pauling entered his new research area only after carefully reviewing the scientific literature. He learned about the amino acids, the building blocks of proteins. Although there were about twenty different amino acids, they all had identical backbones consisting of three atoms: two carbon and one nitrogen.

The problem for scientists, however, was that proteins were huge molecules, made of as many as tens of thousands of atoms. Even Pauling had never figured out the structure of a molecule anywhere nearly that large. In addition, proteins were not very stable. Heat a protein, treat it with a mild acid, or make it react with oxygen—in so doing, you cause the protein to lose its correct shape and properties. This process is called denaturation.

One of Pauling's first significant achievements in bridging chemistry and biology was his work on protein denaturation. He was the first to figure out what denaturation actually did to the structure of proteins. In 1935, he was one of the few American scientists to understand hydrogen bonds. He quickly saw the crucial role hydrogen bonds played in maintaining protein structure. His 1936 paper "On the Structure of Native, Denatured, and Coagulated Proteins" explained the role the chemical bond plays in protein activity and protein denaturation. According to Pauling, proteins were long chains of amino acids hooked together by linkages called peptide bonds. What held proteins in their specific shapes, he argued, were mainly hydrogen bonds between different parts of the peptide chain. As Pauling later summarized, denaturation occurs when the peptide chains lose their "well-defined configuration."[3]

Pauling's early work on the boundary between biology and chemistry also included important research on hemoglobin. Hemoglobin is the protein in red blood cells that makes them red. It carries oxygen and contains iron. An advantage to working with hemoglobin was that it was available in large quantities and could be prepared in nearly pure form from the red blood cells of sheep and cattle. Since it could be crystallized, Pauling at first thought he might uncover its structure through X-ray diffraction. Before long, however, he decided it was too complex a molecule to yield its secrets to that technique.

Pauling was not destined to be the scientist who discovered the structure of hemoglobin. Viennese-born British scientist Max Perutz solved its structure in 1953 and produced a complete model of it in 1959. Perutz's achievement was acknowledged when he was awarded the Nobel Prize in Chemistry in 1962. But what Pauling did learn about hemoglobin would lead him to a major success in bridging chemistry and medicine.

In 1936 Pauling published several papers on the nature of the chemical bonds in hemoglobin. He based these papers on his study of the way the complex hemoglobin molecule was affected in the presence of a magnetic field. Nearly a decade later Pauling's familiarity with hemoglobin led him to discover the first molecular disease. In spring 1945, toward the end of World War II, Pauling was at a committee meeting. The government had charged the experts on the committee to recommend what medical research deserved public funding after the war. Pauling was the only committee member who was not a physician. Over dinner, the subject of sickle cell anemia came up. This blood disease affects many Africans and African Americans.

One of the doctors on the committee explained that the disease got its name from the shape assumed by the diseased red blood cells. A sickle is a short-handled tool with a crescent-shaped blade for cutting grain or tall grass. In healthy individuals, the red blood cells are round, flattened discs. In patients suffering from sickle cell anemia, the red blood cells take on the shape of a crescent or sickle. By clogging small blood vessels, the sickle-shaped cells hamper the red blood cells from performing their task of carrying oxygen. The resulting symptoms include dangerous blood clots and pain.

The doctor describing the disease also mentioned that fewer sickled red blood cells appeared in the blood carried by arteries, which is rich in oxygen, than in the blood carried by the veins, which is depleted of oxygen. The doctor added that no one could explain this difference. Pauling immediately understood that hemoglobin—the molecule that binds oxygen—was likely to be involved in this disease of the red blood cells. He knew that red blood cells are made primarily of hemoglobin and water.

Five years earlier, in 1940, Pauling had proposed that many biological processes could be explained by what he called "molecular complementariness." By this awkward term he meant simply that one molecule fit as snugly as a hand in a glove against or into another molecule with a shape complementary to it. He believed that biological functions were completely dependent on such precise molecular structure. Pauling showed, for example, that an antibody binds to an antigen because their shapes fit together as precisely as a key fits into a lock. An antibody is a protein in the blood that forms as a reaction to the introduction of a foreign substance called an antigen. By neutralizing the antigen, an antibody provides immunity against certain microorganisms or their toxins.

As he sat now at the 1945 meeting of medical experts, Pauling reflected on what he had just heard about oxygen and sickled cells. He figured out that sickling must occur when complementary shapes on different hemoglobin molecules stick together in long chains inside the red blood cells. Enough of these chains could cause the blood cells to twist out of shape. But when oxygen formed a bond with the hemoglobin, the shape of the molecule must change enough to upset the complementariness. Adding oxygen would thus suppress the sickling, while taking it away would enhance the sickling.

Before the 1940s were out, Pauling's research team in Pasadena had figured out the cause of sickle-cell anemia. They discovered that there was a significant difference between the hemoglobin molecules of sickle-cell patients and those of healthy individuals. In 1949, Pauling's group published an important paper, "Sickle Cell Anemia, a Molecular Disease." It clearly demonstrated for the first time that an inherited disease can result from the alteration of a specific molecule. Pauling and Harvey Itano, his coworker, were later awarded the Martin Luther King Award for their research on sickle cell anemia.

Pauling's main research goal on the boundary between chemistry and biology, however, was to determine the structure of proteins. Although Pauling believed that protein structure was far too complex to uncover through X-ray crystallography alone, British scientists believed that by performing X-ray analysis on entire proteins, they would eventually decipher the structures of proteins.

Pauling, by contrast, believed that he could succeed in determining the structure of proteins by finding out as much as possible about the size and shapes of the smaller features that make up a protein. He would then use this knowledge to figure out what kinds of bonds were likely to hold the features together. He would test his ideas by assembling carefully constructed 3-D models. Finally he would compare the models with the X-ray data.

He decided to work on keratin, the tough protein that forms the outer layer of hair, nails, horns, and hoofs. British physicist William Astbury, working at the University of Leeds, had made X-ray diffraction photos of keratin. Astbury's keratin photographs seemed to suggest that chains of polypeptides—peptides containing between 10 and 100 amino acids—were coiled up in some way.

In May 1937 Astbury visited Pasadena. Pauling had a chance to consider his newest X-ray pictures of keratin. Pauling later recalled, "I spent the summer of 1937 in an unsuccessful effort to find a way of coiling a polypeptide chain in three dimensions compatible with [Astbury's photographs]." His inability to do so led Pauling to conclude that "I was making some unjustified assumption about the structural properties of the molecules."[4] Over a decade would elapse before Pauling understood that the problem lay not in his assumptions but in the interpretation of Astbury's X-ray data.

Pauling was eager to become the first scientist to figure out the structure of a complete protein. He was hardly the only such scientist. Famed British crystallographer William Lawrence Bragg was also at the head of a major research group with the same goal. Bragg, now head of Britain's greatest center for physics—the Cavendish Laboratory at Cambridge, England—had already lost one race to Pauling. It was Pauling's Rules, after all, not Bragg's, that explained the structure of crystals.

In 1948 Pauling spent six months in England at the University of Oxford, where he was the Eastman Professor. He began to think again about the polypeptide chains in keratin. He later recalled how he came back to the problem on which he had last worked in 1937. He had been lying ill with a sinus infection in his Oxford house. "The first day I read detective stories and just tried to keep from feeling miserable, and the second day, too. But I got bored with that, so I thought, 'Why don't I think about the structure of proteins?'"[5]

As a visual aid, he used a ruler and pencil to sketch amino acid chains on paper. He placed bonds at the distances and

LINUS AND AVA HELEN WATCH AS THEIR CHILDREN, LINDA, CRELLIN, LINUS, JR., AND PETER (LEFT TO RIGHT) PLAY WITH THEIR PET RABBITS IN 1941.

angles that he dredged up from his memory. As he fiddled around with the 3-D models, he realized that one shape made sense: a spiral, similar in shape to a toy Slinky. At first he was so delighted with his discovery that he momentarily "forgot all about having a cold."[6] Soon, however, he realized that the spiral—or helix—was unlikely to produce X-ray patterns that would match those of Astbury's photos. So Pauling kept his thoughts to himself.

Already concerned that Bragg's group would beat him to the finish line, Pauling was distressed when a paper from the Cavendish appeared in spring 1950. By this time, he was back at work in Pasadena. As he read through the paper, however, he realized that only its title gave him cause for worry. Though the paper was called "Polypeptide Chain Configurations in Crystalline Proteins," the suggestions it proposed for possible structures were all flawed when viewed from a chemist's perspective.

Pauling took up the protein work again with renewed vigor. Using wire, balls, and sticks, he built models of likely structures. The helix still seemed to be the most appealing structure. Although it still did not agree with Astbury's photos, the race with Bragg's group was too close, so he decided to take a risk. In October 1950, he submitted a preliminary paper for publication. In it he proposed his helix model.

The risk paid off. By spring 1951, Pauling had submitted a series of papers that rocked the world of protein research. Pauling demonstrated that the so-called alpha helix was the main structural element in hair and fingernails, as well as horns and hoofs. The alpha helix would soon be shown to be an important structural feature of hemoglobin and several other proteins also.

Pauling's discovery of the alpha helix brought him international fame. In September 1951, *Life* magazine featured a large photo of Pauling explaining his model of the alpha helix. The headline read "Chemists Solve a Great Mystery."

Although Bragg was once more the victim of Pauling's oneupsmanship, he sent Pauling a gracious congratulatory note "on what I feel is a very real and vital advance toward the understanding of proteins."[7] Bragg did not quickly get over the alpha helix "fiasco," as James Watson, a young American postdoctoral fellow at the Cavendish later explained. "It hurt his pride at a tender point. There had been previous encounters with Pauling, stretching over a twenty-five-year interval. All too often Linus had got there first."[8]

Bragg's group, however, would soon have their day in the sun at Pauling's expense. In the early 1950s the scientific study of heredity, or genetics, was still in its early stages. Most geneticists believed that nucleic acids—complex compounds found in all living cells—were less likely to determine individual hereditary characteristics than proteins were. Nonetheless, Pauling decided to work on the structure of DNA, one of the nucleic acids. Although the nucleic acids also consisted of long chains of molecules, their structures seemed to be less complicated than those of proteins. Pauling thought it should be comparatively easy to work out the structure of DNA using his model-building method. He did not consider the structure of DNA worthy of his full professional attention, however.

Again, Astbury had X-ray diffraction photos of DNA,

but they provided little useful data. London-based researcher Maurice Wilkins had some better photos. Wilkins, however, was worried that if he shared his photos with Pauling, the American would uncover DNA's structure before he and his talented crystallographer colleague Rosalind Franklin succeeded in doing so. So he denied Pauling access to them.

Pauling would probably have been given permission to see those pictures if he had been able to attend a meeting of protein researchers in England in May 1952. Because Pauling's political activities were suspect in the eyes of the American government, however, the State Department refused to give Pauling a passport. Despite Pauling's attempt to reverse this decision by writing President Truman himself, he was not issued a passport until July 1952, after the protein research meeting had taken place.

Pauling nevertheless used his new passport to attend some scientific meetings that summer in France. At the second meeting he learned that recent research had confirmed that DNA, not a protein, was the crucial genetic molecule.

Despite the revelation, proteins were still the main topic on Pauling's mind while he was abroad. After the meetings in France, Pauling went to England but made no effort to see Wilkins's and Franklin's DNA photos.

Pauling believed he could be the first to solve the structure of DNA. He had little respect for the depth of Franklin's and Wilkins's backgrounds in chemistry. He knew that at the Cavendish Laboratory young James Watson and his colleague, British graduate student Francis Crick, were working on DNA. They did not seem much of a threat, however. Bragg's research teams had not succeeded in besting Pauling to date.

On this occasion, Pauling was to be beaten by Watson and Crick, who used the Pauling method of model-building based on chemical principles. James Watson later recalled his and Crick's battle plan: They would "imitate Linus Pauling and beat him at his own game."[9] They wanted to show the world "that Pauling was not the only one capable of true insight into how biological molecules were constructed."[10]

Pauling took up serious work on DNA only in late autumn 1952. By that time, it was clear that while his alpha helix discovery was important, it was not as big a break-through as the discovery of the structure of DNA would be. Pauling quickly came up with a structure for DNA that seemed to fit most of the X-ray data. It was a triple helix. He wrote his second son, Peter, then a graduate student at the Cavendish, and Jerry Donohue, a Caltech crystallographer on leave there. He told them that he would shortly publish a paper on the structure of nucleic acids.

Just after Christmas 1952, Pauling submitted a paper called "A Proposed Structure for the Nucleic Acids." He rushed it into print because he wanted to be the one to get credit for cracking the code of life. He never made his own X-ray photos of DNA, and he never built 3-D models of his triple helix.

Watson and Crick had been dejected to learn from Peter Pauling of his father's upcoming publication. When they read the manuscript Pauling sent to Peter, their dejection turned to astonishment and then glee. As Watson later wrote, "At once I felt something was not right."[11] Watson and Crick quickly saw that Pauling—of all people—had made some basic mistakes in the chemistry underlying his proposed structure. "If a student had made a similar mistake," wrote Watson, "he would be thought unfit to benefit from Cal Tech's chemistry faculty."[12] When they shared the surprising news with their colleagues, one of them "expressed pleasure that a giant had forgotten elementary college chemistry."[13] And this giant was the author of the most widely used introductory chemistry textbook for college students!

Quickly realizing that "smiling too long over [Pauling's] mistake might be fatal," Watson and Crick returned to their work. Bragg gave them his blessing to pursue the DNA research single-mindedly.[14]

In April 1953 Watson and Crick submitted a paper presenting a different model for the structure of DNA. It was a double, not triple, helix. They had clearly benefited from Pauling's work on "molecular complementariness," however. Each of the strands of their double helix was complementary to the other. On its own, each could form a new double helix identical to the original one.

Just as Bragg had always graciously complimented Pauling's achievements when Pauling had beaten Bragg, Pauling took an early public opportunity to admit that his proposed structure for DNA was wrong and the Cavendish model correct. At a scientific meeting later in the spring of 1953, Pauling said, "I think that we must admit that [the triple helix] is probably wrong. Although some refinement might be made, I feel that it is very likely that the Watson-Crick structure is essentially correct."[15]

In 1962 Watson and Crick shared the Nobel Prize for

medicine for their work on uncovering the structure of DNA. (It was a good year for Bragg's group, since Max Perutz and John Kendrew, also of the Cavendish, won the Nobel Prize for Chemistry that year for their work on hemoglobin and the related protein, myoglobin.) If Pauling had been the one to figure out the structure of DNA, presumably he would have won the Nobel Prize for that discovery too.

How upset was Pauling by his DNA misstep? At the age of ninety, he wrote about his failure to get a third Nobel prize. In his comment he did not refer specifically to the DNA research, but perhaps the comment reveals all the same that he was satisfied with what he had accomplished: "People have said to me that if I hadn't received the Nobel Prize in Chemistry probably I would have received the Nobel Prize in Medicine for the discovery of molecular diseases. Perhaps so. But it doesn't bother me. Why should I discover everything? I'm satisfied."[16]

CHAPTER SEVEN

PATRIOT OR TRAITOR?

The development of the atom bomb during World War II transformed Pauling into a political activist. In early 1943 he was approached by J. Robert Oppenheimer, the director of the secret government-sponsored Manhattan Project to develop an atomic bomb. Oppenheimer wanted Pauling to direct the project's chemistry division. Pauling declined— "Not because I felt that it was wrong to work on the development of nuclear weapons, rather that I had other jobs that I was doing."[1]

Those other jobs were different from Pauling's usual areas of research. Like other scientists, he turned his laboratories over to work that could hasten the victory of the United States and its allies in the war. He devised the Pauling Oxygen Analyzer to measure the level of oxygen in submarines. His laboratory helped develop improved fuels for American rockets. He also developed a type of synthetic blood plasma (the fluid portion of blood) that could be used in emergencies for transfusions in clinics at the front.

Once a month he made the long three-day train trip to Washington, D.C., as a wartime scientific consultant to the government. In 1948 President Harry S. Truman bestowed the Presidential Medal for Merit on Pauling "for outstanding services to the United States from October 1940 to June 1946."[2]

Pauling's war work did not protect him and his family from being persecuted for acting on their political beliefs a few months before the war ended, however. The United States had entered the war in December 1941 following the surprise Japanese attack on the U.S. military base in Pearl Harbor, Honolulu. In one of the more shameful episodes in American history, large numbers of loyal Americans of Japanese ancestry who lived on the west coast of the United States were rounded up in 1942 and sent to internment camps. In March 1945 the Paulings agreed to hire as a short-term gardener a young Japanese-American who had been released from a camp and would soon be inducted into the army. After the young man's departure, the Paulings' fourteen-year-old son, Peter, found threatening graffiti scrawled on the family's garage door. Anonymous phone calls and hate mail followed. When Pauling left for his next consulting trip to Washington, an armed guard was assigned to protect the family. The identity of those who issued the threats was never revealed.

In early August 1945, Pauling was surprised to discover that Oppenheimer's Manhattan Project had succeeded in its goal. On August 7, the United States dropped an atomic bomb on the Japanese city Hiroshima. Three days later, the U.S. dropped a second bomb on Nagasaki. Shortly thereafter the Japanese surrendered.

Although everyone was elated that the war was finally over, many scientists, including Pauling, began to feel responsible for the destructive power unleashed by the new weapons that scientists had developed. Pauling later recalled how the dawning of the nuclear age transformed him. In 1945, inspired by Ava Helen, he made the momentous decision "to sacrifice part of my scientific career to working for the control of nuclear weapons and for the achievement of world peace."[3]

In 1946 Pauling was asked by Albert Einstein, the famous physicist, to join the Emergency Committee of Atomic Scientists. Its aim was to help the public understand the unprecedented destructive power of nuclear weapons. Pauling later remembered, "Before then I had made some public talks about nuclear weapons and nuclear war; but it was Einstein's example that inspired my wife and me to devote energy and effort to pacifist activities."[4] He and Ava Helen also joined other groups that promoted world peace.

When Pauling first began to speak out about nuclear war, Ava Helen criticized his lectures: "you give the audience the impression that you are not sure about what you are saying." Pauling called Ava Helen's remark "an episode that changed my life." He decided to study "international relations, international law, treaties, histories, the peace movement, and other subjects relating to the whole question of how to abolish war from the world and to achieve the goal of a peaceful world."[5] In late 1947, on board the ship taking him to England for a semester, Pauling scrawled the following resolution on the back of a piece of cardboard: "In every lecture that I give from now on, every public lecture, I pledge to make some mention of the need for world peace."[6]

Unfortunately, Pauling's political views were developing in a hostile Cold War environment. The Soviet Union developed its first atomic weapon in the late 1940s. From then on, the U.S. and the Soviet Union were involved in an arms race. Each side was bent on developing new, more powerful nuclear weapons to keep the other side from attacking.

The Federal Bureau of Investigation (FBI) began keeping files on Americans who joined groups that promoted world peace. Such individuals were suspected of being Communists or at least Communist sympathizers. For over twenty years, the FBI considered Pauling a threat to national security. When the bureau finally closed its investigation of Pauling in 1972, nothing in the 2500-page file it had gathered on him indicated that he had ever been a Communist.

> "[I decided] to sacrifice part of my scientific career to working for the control of nuclear weapons and for the achievement of world peace."
>
> —Linus Pauling

Pauling was able to outsmart some of those who would punish him for his views. For example, he was informed in the early 1950s that the National Science Foundation and the National Institutes of Health were withdrawing support for some of his research. Pauling resubmitted the grant applications in the names of his scientific collaborators. Since these researchers had done nothing to put themselves on the FBI's radar screen, the resubmitted grant applications were approved.

Other run-ins with government agencies were less easily resolved. During the 1950s the State Department made international travel difficult for Pauling by denying him a passport. In addition to his inability to attend the protein conference in England in May 1952, he was denied a passport to dedicate a scientific institute in India in summer 1954. Pauling later told an interviewer, "for two years, the State Department caused trouble for me. They wouldn't tell me why—they said not in the best interest of the United States, or your anti-Communist statements haven't been strong enough."[7]

Ironically, while the American government was growing increasingly concerned that Pauling was a Communist, the Communist scientific authorities wanted nothing to do with Pauling's science. An important part of Pauling's quantum mechanical approach to molecular structure is his theory of resonance. According to this theory, some substances, such as benzene, cannot be described in terms of a single structure. Pauling argued that the benzene molecule must be described as fluctuating, or resonating, between two structures at the same time.

Pauling later explained, "around 1949 there was issued an attack on me in the Soviet Union saying that the theory of resonance is incompatible with [Communist ideology]. There was a meeting of 800 chemists in Moscow where they got up one after the other, many of them, and promised never again to use the theory of resonance in their teaching or publications." Although like other scientists around the world, the Soviet scientists had been accustomed to using resonance theory, they now were forced to acknowledge "the error of [their] ways."[8]

In the mid-1950s, Pauling broadened his political message. He warned his audiences not only about the dangers of a major nuclear war but also about the effects on their health that resulted from the testing of nuclear weapons. Pauling began to speak about radioactive fallout—the tiny but damaging particles that were released into the atmosphere following a nuclear explosion. Even though nuclear weapons were tested in remote areas, winds and clouds carried around the world the particles released during the explosions. When the fallout settled, it contaminated Earth's air, ground, and water.

In 1958 Pauling published a book, *No More War!* It summarized the views he expressed in his anti-war lectures. He explained how radioactive fallout could damage cells in the human body. The possible results included a rise in the number of cases of both cancer and birth defects. He also belittled the government's claim that the population could survive nuclear war and protect itself against fallout by taking refuge in underground concrete fallout shelters.

Not all scientists agreed with Pauling's arguments. Many believed that Americans and the entire free world would be safer if the government continued to develop nuclear weapons that would deter the Communist bloc from attacking. They did not deny that radiation caused damage but argued that Americans were exposed to much more radiation from chest X-rays and other medical procedures than from fallout. Pauling's critics also said that the exposure to fallout would increase each individual's chance of developing cancer only by a tiny amount. Given the threat of Communism, they believed that the danger from radioactive fallout was small and acceptable.

Pauling, however, argued that while the risk to each person was small, in terms of the entire population it was unacceptable. Thousands of additional people would be born with birth defects and thousands would die of cancer because of exposure to fallout.

Earlier in 1958 Pauling presented to the Secretary-General of the United Nations a petition to end nuclear war. It had been signed by thousands of scientists from over forty countries. The petition effort had begun the previous spring at Washington University in St. Louis. Pauling had lectured there on "Science in the Modern World." Stimulated by Pauling's words about the dangers of radioactive fallout, a group of scientists met with Pauling

LINUS AND AVA HELEN PAULING LEAD A LOS ANGELES PEACE MARCH IN 1960.

that afternoon to write up a petition. By evening, the petitions were ready to send out. The petition read, in part: "We, the scientists whose names are signed below, urge that an international agreement to stop the testing of nuclear bombs be made now. . . . We deem it imperative that immediate action be taken to effect an international agreement to stop the testing of all nuclear weapons."[9]

Pauling was careful not to use Caltech staff or money to circulate the petition. With his own money he hired a part-time secretary to type, copy, and mail the petition, as well as to arrange for translating it into other languages.

In 1960, over two years after presenting the petition at the United Nations, Pauling was called to testify before a subcommittee of the United States Senate. The Senate Internal Security Subcommittee (SISS) wanted to know how Pauling had succeeded in getting all the signatures on his petition. They believed he must have had the support of a large organization—probably a Communist one. The senators asked him to name those individuals who had helped him circulate the petition. Pauling refused to reveal any names, even though he knew he might end up in prison if the Senate charged him with contempt.

Overcoming whatever fear he might have felt, Pauling said, "I think that my reputation and example may well have led these younger people to work for peace in this way [by circulating the petition]. My conscience will not allow me to protect myself by sacrificing these idealistic and hopeful people, and I am not going to do it. As a matter of conscience, as a matter of principle, as a matter of morality, I have decided that I shall not conform to the request of the subcommittee."[10]

The senators finally dismissed Pauling without extracting any names from him. They did, however, issue a report that included sections on Pauling's "Associations with Individuals with Known Communist Records" and his "Opposition to Anti-Communist Legislation and Measures."

Two years later Pauling again demonstrated the courage of his convictions in a less threatening encounter. President John F. Kennedy, elected in November 1960, and his wife, Jacqueline, had included the Paulings in a dinner invitation for April 29, 1962. Among the 175 guests were other distinguished and creative Americans, including 48 other Nobel laureates. Pauling was pleased to accept his first invitation to the White House. Nonetheless he participated in a peace march around the presidential home. He carried a placard urging both the American leader and his British counterpart that "We Have No Right to Test."

When the forty-four-year-old president greeted the sixty-year-old scientist at the dinner, Kennedy expressed his admiration for Pauling's courage. Mrs. Kennedy told him that their four-year-old daughter, Caroline, had watched the demonstration and asked, "Mummy, what has Daddy done wrong now?"[11]

Pauling's efforts to end nuclear testing finally paid off. On August 5, 1963, the United States and the Soviet Union signed the world's first nuclear test-ban treaty. They agreed to end tests of nuclear weapons not only in the atmosphere but also in outer space and under the ocean. (Underground testing was not ruled out, however.) The treaty was to go into effect on October 10, 1963. On that day the Nobel Prize committee of the Norwegian Parliament announced that Pauling had been granted the

Peace Prize for the previous year, when none had been awarded. Pauling was deeply gratified.

Pauling was often asked which of his two Nobel Prizes he valued more. Sometimes he said, "I am equally proud of both endeavors," which represented his "accomplishments in both science and humanism."[12] On other occasions he said, "Well, I was happy to receive the Nobel Prize for Chemistry, but I had just been having a good time carrying out studies in the field of chemistry and trying to make discoveries. The Nobel Peace Prize is the one I value more because it means . . . that I have been doing my duty to my fellow human beings."[13]

Similarly, when asked which of his achievements instilled in him the most pride, he reported, "Sometimes I say I'm most proud of my 1931 paper, which changed the nature of chemistry in a significant way. Sometimes . . . I say . . . contributions to well-being [made by] my work in the effort to get a bomb test treaty signed, stopping damage by fallout."[14]

CHAPTER EIGHT

IN SEARCH OF
A NEW HOME

Pauling was certainly proud of becoming the first person to win two unshared Nobel prizes. Nonetheless, the announcement of his second Nobel prize thrust him into a decade filled with turmoil and dissatisfaction.

Late in his life, in an introduction to a collection of his "writings, speeches, and interviews," Pauling wrote, "I have not regretted my peace activism, although this has damaged my reputation as a scientist among certain people and institutions."[1] Most painfully, he watched the damage to his reputation grow at Caltech. Some of the damage was, indeed, related to Pauling's peace work. Even before he won the chemistry prize in 1954, two important trustees resigned because of Pauling's outspoken anti-nuclear stance. As Pauling later explained, "The trustees [of Caltech], of course, were mainly business men and conservative and supporters of the Cold War, and they seemed to consider that working for peace between the United States and the

Soviet Union was in some way subversive. . . . So, the trustees tried to get the Institute to fire me."[2]

The president of Caltech, Lee DuBridge, understood he could not simply fire a tenured professor. But in 1958, the year Pauling delivered the nuclear test ban petition to the United Nations, Caltech removed him from his position as chairman of the division of chemistry and chemical engineering. He had held the position for twenty years. Although Pauling remained on the faculty, his salary was reduced.

Part of the dissatisfaction with Pauling at Caltech, however, was scientific. Around 1955 Pauling became interested in mental diseases. It occurred to him that perhaps mental disorders were also molecular diseases that resulted from abnormally structured molecules. He received a large grant from the Ford Foundation to do the work. His research program called for analyzing urine and blood. He also did work on a molecular theory of general anesthesia. To test his ideas on this subject, his researchers used goldfish as test animals. Many of his colleagues in the chemistry division were dismayed. What did this kind of work have to do with traditional chemistry? Why should Pauling's fringe projects take up so much lab space when other, more serious researchers could put it to better use? In the meantime, fewer chemists were utilizing Pauling's model of the chemical bond than the rival model of his colleague Robert Mulliken. (Mulliken's "molecular orbital theory" did not disprove Pauling's model but provided a different mathematical approach to analyzing chemical bonds by quantum mechanics.)

Besides, Pauling seemed to be spending very little time

in Pasadena. He was always off somewhere else, doing what he must have considered more important than teaching his classes, supervising the research in his labs, or interacting with his colleagues. In 1963 a new chairman of the division of chemistry and chemical engineering began to reduce Pauling's lab space. Pauling later said, when "they began interfering with my research projects, . . . I decided that I was going to have to leave the Institute."[3]

What actually prompted his resignation, however, was DuBridge's reaction to his peace prize. As he told the interviewer, "I found . . . that the president had stated to the *Los Angeles Times* . . . that it was pretty remarkable for any person to receive two Nobel Prizes, but there was much difference of opinion about the value of the work that Professor Pauling had done. . . . I wasn't happy about leaving the Institute, but I did leave."[4] Officially, however, Pauling was merely taking a leave of absence from Caltech to become a resident professor of physical and biological sciences at the Center for the Study of Democratic Institutions (CSDI) in Santa Barbara, California.

There were other upheavals in Pauling's life at about the same time. In 1962 he had brought a libel lawsuit against William F. Buckley's conservative journal, *The National Review*. Buckley had called Pauling "a megaphone of Soviet policy," and had accused him of lending "his name, energy, voice and pen to one after another Soviet-serving enterprise."[5] It was the first of many similar suits that Pauling filed. In 1966 the judge hearing the case dismissed it. He ruled that Pauling "has added the prestige of his reputation to aid the causes in which he believes." In doing so, argued the judge, "he also limited his legal remedies for any claimed libel of his reputation. And perhaps this can be deemed another sacrifice that he is making for the things he believes in."[6]

While Pauling "didn't like" the judge's decision and "didn't like having my libel suit fail," he agreed that it was "a good decision." He reached that conclusion because "people who want to discuss important questions need to be free to mention what other well-known people have said and perhaps to criticize them."[7]

He was less forgiving, however, of the American Chemical Society (ACS). He had been the society's president in 1949, and he expected the society's congratulations on the occasion of his second Nobel prize. The *Journal of the American Chemical Society*, however, where he had published much of his pathbreaking research, basically ignored the award. It included only a single mention of it in the back pages of one issue. Pauling resigned his membership in the ACS at the end of 1963.

Another major disruption in Pauling's life was the move from his custom-designed home in Pasadena. The house stayed in the family, as the Paulings' daughter, Linda, who had married a Caltech geologist, Barclay Kamb, bought the home for her own family. Linus and Ava Helen moved to a small house in Santa Barbara, near CSDI.

Santa Barbara would not be his home for long, however. Pauling would be a nomad for the next decade, moving from one institution to another. He quickly became disenchanted with CSDI. He scribbled himself an undated note, "My complaint about the Center is that the great amount of talk leads to little in the way of accepted conclusions."[8]

Worse, Pauling found that he was being denied grant money because he had no lab at the center. A former student, now chair of the chemistry department at the University of California at Santa Barbara, tried to work out an appointment for Pauling there. But the chancellor of the university refused to endorse the appointment because of Pauling's political activities. Luckily, Pauling was able to carry out some theoretical work at CSDI. But his new theory on the structure of the atomic nucleus was not regarded with much interest by either chemists or physicists.

In 1967, during a year's leave of absence from CSDI, Pauling left the center for good. He took a position at the University of California at San Diego (UCSD). Ava Helen found them a house in La Jolla, the suburb where the university is based. He hoped to advance his work on mental health there. In late 1966 and early 1967, Pauling worked out a theory he called "orthomolecular psychiatry." In his first publication on the topic he explained what he meant by that term: "I believe that mental disease . . . is caused by . . . abnormal molecular concentrations of essential substances."[9] Pauling soon expanded his theory to include not only mental illness but also all other diseases. To test his theory, he needed a lab.

His initial appointment at UCSD was only a year's visiting professorship of chemistry and physics. But the chemistry department expressed interest in making the visit the prelude to a permanent appointment. He did not find professional satisfaction at San Diego, however. Once again his political views got in his way. The United States was now embroiled in the controversial war in Vietnam. Pauling's active participation in the antiwar movement did not escape the notice of the university's administration. Although Pauling remained at UCSD for a second year, he was not reappointed a third time.

The Paulings moved yet again, this time to Stanford University. Located in Palo Alto, California, Stanford was closer to the Paulings' country house, Deer Flat Ranch, which they had purchased with the 1954 Nobel prize money. But the appointment was far from ideal. Pauling had to pay half his salary and all his expenses from research grants. Neither his office nor his lab was in the chemistry building. A janitor's closet in the chemical engineering building was hastily converted into an office for his secretary. The small lab he had in that building was reclaimed by the chemical engineering department in 1973.

> "I believe that mental disease . . . is caused by . . . abnormal molecular concentrations of essential substances."
>
> —Linus Pauling

When Pauling moved from UCSD to Stanford, he was followed by a younger researcher, Arthur B. Robinson. Robinson had done brilliant undergraduate work in biochemistry at Caltech. His doctoral work at UCSD had been so impressive that UCSD hired him as soon as he completed it. Pauling and Robinson began to collaborate on Pauling's orthomolecular work while Pauling was at UCSD.

By 1972 it was clear to Pauling and Robinson that they needed more lab space for their research. They asked Stanford to build them a new building. They offered to raise money to fund part of the construction. Reminding

Pauling that he was past retirement age, Stanford turned down his request.

In spring 1973 Pauling and Robinson announced that they were setting up their own research institute. The Institute of Orthomolecular Medicine (IOM) was located in Menlo Park, a few miles from Stanford. Pauling had thought of setting up an institute of his own as early as 1960. He had given up the idea at that time, however, when he discovered how much money it would take to make such an institute viable. Finding funding would be an ongoing concern at the Linus Pauling Institute (LPI), as the IOM was renamed in 1974.

The main focus of research at the LPI was the outcome of an experience Pauling had in 1966. In March of that year, he was awarded a medal for his work bridging biology and medicine. During his lecture at the award ceremony, Pauling—now sixty-five—remarked that he hoped he would live another fifteen or twenty years so that he could see the new advances in medicine that were sure to follow. A biochemist in the audience, Irwin Stone, wrote Pauling a letter. He told Pauling he might prolong his life for up to fifty years if he followed Stone's advice on vitamin C. Stone recommended taking a megadose of the vitamin—a much larger amount than the recommended daily allowance (RDA) that the government had established for ascorbic acid (another name for vitamin C). At the time, the RDA was sixty milligrams; in 1974, it was lowered to forty-five milligrams.

Pauling had had a previous successful experience with vitamin and dietary therapy twenty-five years earlier. In March 1941, shortly after his fortieth birthday, he was diagnosed with Bright's disease, a serious kidney ailment. Pauling later attributed his survival to the diet prescribed by Dr. Thomas Addis, a California kidney specialist. In addition to limiting his intake of protein and salt, the diet stressed grains, fruit, and vegetables, along with water and supplemental vitamins and minerals.

Following Stone's suggestion, Pauling began taking three grams (3,000 milligrams) of vitamin C daily—fifty times more than the RDA of 0.06 grams (60 milligrams). He noticed a decline in the number of colds he was used to having. Although he felt better in general than he had in

IN THIS 1976 PHOTO, LINUS PAULING STANDS BETWEEN SON CRELLIN (LEFT) AND GRANDSON BARCLAY J. KAMB. STANDING IN FRONT OF THEM ARE ANTHONY KAMB, AVA HELEN PAULING, LINUS KAMB, LINDA PAULING KAMB, AND LINUS PAULING, JR. (LEFT TO RIGHT).

years, he kept the information to himself for three years. Then in late 1969, during a talk he gave to physicians, he mentioned his success with vitamin C megadoses to prevent colds. Several newspapers ran stories on Pauling's comment.

The newspaper coverage led to another unexpected letter in Pauling's mail. Dr. Victor Herbert, who helped establish the RDA for vitamins, wrote to criticize Pauling. He accused the Nobel laureate of aiding and abetting those "quacks" who convinced Americans to waste their money on ineffective vitamin therapy. Why were there no careful research studies to support Pauling's claim that vitamin C had an effect on colds, asked Herbert? Pauling later explained that Herbert was "in a sense . . . responsible for my having spent more than twenty years in this vitamin field. He irritated me so much . . . that I sat down and wrote my book *Vitamin C and the Common Cold*."[10]

As he approached seventy, Pauling thus set out on another controversial crusade. This time his goal was to prove that vitamin C could do wonders for human health. In the introduction to *Vitamin C and the Common Cold*, Pauling described his work beginning in 1935 on "molecular structure of the substances present in the human body." He went on to explain how that research had alerted him to the importance of vitamins, and how "for some people, at any rate, improved health might result from an increase in intake of certain vitamins." He held out hope that "improvement of the nutrition of the people by an adequate intake of ascorbic acid" might eventually control, if not eliminate, the common cold in the United States.[11]

Pauling's fame helped make the book an enormous success. Sales of vitamin C in the United States skyrocketed. In

1971 the book was singled out by the Phi Beta Kappa Society, the honorary scholastic fraternity, as one of the most significant books published the previous year. Most nutritionists and physicians, however, dismissed the book. They argued that Pauling misinterpreted data. Where he saw significant effects of vitamin C, experts saw none. Pauling might be a brilliant chemist, they insisted, but his claims about the efficacy of taking vitamin megadoses remained unconfirmed.

In his chemistry research, Pauling had always followed up on his intuition by performing careful experiments. Now he was making claims about nutrition that simply lacked the proof needed to confirm them. Administrators at Stanford, where Pauling was now working, also frowned on Pauling's new obsession with vitamin C. To them and to others he was beginning to seem less like a serious scientist.

Before long Pauling would extend his claims about the health benefits of vitamin C megadoses. In 1976 he published an expanded version of his book, which included the supposed benefits of vitamin C in treating not only the common cold but also the flu. Much more controversial were Pauling's claims about vitamin C and cancer.

In November 1971 Pauling received a letter from Dr. Ewan Cameron, a surgeon from Scotland. Cameron claimed that he had successfully use large doses of vitamin C on cancer patients in his Vale of Leven Hospital. Impressed with Cameron's work, Pauling suggested they collaborate on an article. The subtitle of their paper was "An Orthomolecular Approach to Treatment of Cancer and Other Diseases." They decided to submit it to the Proceedings of the National Academy of Sciences (PNAS).

Pauling had been a member of the elite academy since 1933.

As the academy's journal, PNAS had an unusual editorial policy. Scientific journals routinely sent out authors' papers for review by other scientists. But PNAS assumed that scientists good enough to be admitted to the academy were good enough to have their work published without such a review. In 1972, however, Pauling's paper with Cameron became the first paper by a member of the academy to be refused for publication in PNAS. The journal's editorial board argued that cancer treatment papers should be published in medical journals that could properly evaluate their worth. Pauling and Cameron rewrote the paper, toning down their recommendations for vitamin C therapy. The journal rejected it a second time. Eventually, a publication for cancer specialists, *Oncology*, agreed to publish the joint paper.

Pauling's work with Cameron was on the list of research projects that would be carried out at the Linus Pauling Institute. As they moved from Stanford to their own premises, Robinson and Pauling had high hopes for their new institute. They were confident that their health research would be funded by the government. They even dreamed of eventually offering advanced degrees at LPI.

CHAPTER NINE

INDUSTRIOUS TO THE END

In his 1986 bestselling book *How to Live Longer and Feel Better,* Pauling gave the following advice: "Avoid stress. Work at a job that you like. Be happy with your family."[1] In his last twenty years, Pauling was unable to avoid stress. He suffered a terrible loss in his family life. But until the very end he worked at a job that he clearly loved.

These years witnessed the mending of some previously damaged bridges linking Pauling to governments and to scientific institutions. His achievements were once again recognized by his own country. In 1975 President Gerald R. Ford awarded Pauling the National Medal of Science. The president's science advisor explained that "the award is part of a mood of conciliation throughout our nation. . . . We disagree on politics pretty strongly at times, but science is science, and what Pauling has done in science has been of importance to all the people of the world."[2] (Nonetheless, a conservative publication denounced the award as "another a-Pauling Ford action."[3])

The following year Pauling was amused to note how his reputation had improved at the FBI. A biochemist at the University of California at Berkeley told him that he had been seated on a plane next to a man who eventually identified himself as an FBI agent. The agent asked the biochemist if he knew Pauling. Not sure what would come next, the biochemist admitted they were acquainted. "Now there's a really great scientist," said the agent. "I owe a lot to him. Now I [no longer have] bad colds."[4]

Despite his improved relationship with the U.S. government, Pauling continued to speak out against national policy when it seemed wrong to him. At the age of ninety, for example, he drafted an open letter to President George H. W. Bush opposing the Gulf War. He also paid for an advertisement in *The New York Times* and a second in a Washington, D.C., newspaper, urging the U.S. to rely on diplomacy instead of war.

The Soviet Union, which had previously rejected Pauling's theory of resonance, also took official notice of his achievements. In 1978 Pauling received the highest award of the Soviet Academy of Science, the Lomonosov Gold Medal.

Three scientific institutions that had slighted Pauling in the recent past also made amends. In 1976 the American Chemical Society, from which Pauling had resigned in 1963, invited him to give the keynote address on the occasion of the society's 100th birthday. In 1984 the society bestowed upon him its most prestigious honor, the Priestley Medal.

Similarly, in September 1978, the *Proceedings of the National Academy of Sciences* published a joint paper in which Pauling and Cameron summarized their newly reconsidered results. (A member of the editorial board, however, included a note, which emphasized his reservations about the way the researchers had designed the study.) The following year Pauling became the first person to receive the society's medal in the chemical sciences.

Perhaps most meaningful for Pauling was the affection and respect he found once again at Caltech. The institute organized symposia in honor of Pauling's eighty-fifth and ninetieth birthdays. In 1992 a book containing the talks delivered at the second symposium was published. Called *The Chemical Bond: Structure and Dynamics*, the book was dedicated "To Linus Pauling, one of the greatest scientists of the twentieth century." The introduction spoke volumes: "Linus and Caltech are one institution, only ten years apart in age, and the bond between them is very strong. Since our first celebration in 1986, we now have at Caltech the Linus Pauling Lectureship, the Linus Pauling Professorship, and the Linus Pauling Lecture Hall."[5]

Nonetheless, the last two decades of Pauling's life were riddled with stress, both professional and personal. His high hopes for the Linus Pauling Institute (LPI) were not realized. Arthur Robinson had been named president and director of the institute in summer 1975. He held those titles for less than four years before Pauling ousted him. Not only was Robinson a poor administrator, but Pauling also took strong exception to his handling of an anticancer research study.

Unfortunately for the LPI, Pauling himself had set an example by attempting to settle disputes through lawsuits. Robinson filed eight such suits. By 1983, after five years, the board of the LPI decided to settle out of court. During those five years, however, the institute's reputation suffered, and all the funds it raised went towards legal fees. In 1981 the LPI had to relocate to a renovated warehouse in Palo Alto. It suffered another financial setback in 1991.

Despite the less than ideal conditions, however, the institute's researchers published over 500 papers and books in the two decades between 1974 and 1994. The LPI also held scientific conferences from time to time.

Pauling's major focus at the LPI was his work with Cameron on the benefits of vitamin C in treating cancer. Their collaboration was harmonious, but the reaction of funding agencies and the medical establishment to their work was a source of distress to Pauling. In 1979 Pauling and Cameron published a book, *Cancer and Vitamin C*, about the role of vitamin C in cancer treatment. That year they also published an article in *Cancer Research*. Stressing the "evidence . . . that . . . cancer evokes an increased requirement for ascorbic acid," they called for immediate studies on the vitamin's role in preventing and treating cancer.[6]

They were disappointed, however, with the results of a National Cancer Institute (NCI) study that seemed to refute their ideas. Pauling noted that the NCI study, unlike Cameron's, had included some patients who had been treated with extensive chemotherapy before the vitamin C therapy began. It was not an easy matter for him to convince the NCI to fund a second study to correct this problem.

When the results of the second study were released in 1985, they also showed that vitamin C treatment of cancer was ineffective. An NCI official called the results "definitive."[7] Pauling detected an error in this study, too. When the researchers did not find any improvement in the patients' condition, they took them off the vitamin C treatment. Pauling argued that such rapid withdrawal of vitamin C megadoses could cause the patients' level of the vitamin to plummet. According to Pauling, the NCI study might actually have hastened the patients' deaths.

Pauling, now eighty-four, publicized what he saw as the flaws in the study in any way he could. His lawyer convinced him not to sue those responsible for the study. He was unsuccessful in getting the topic reevaluated.

In 1989, however, a new director took over at the NCI. Some months after the director and Pauling had a lengthy conversation, the NCI announced it would cosponsor an international symposium on vitamin C and cancer later in 1990. Pauling shortly thereafter described the conference and his reaction to it: "forty scientists presented papers on vitamin C and cancer. . . . The National Cancer Institute has now set up a panel of physicians to examine the case histories of the patients that my associate Dr. Cameron has sent in to them. . . . So it looks hopeful in this respect. The National Cancer Institute is also carrying out studies on the value of increased intake of vitamin C in preventing cancer. . . . I regret that it took sixteen years to get the National Cancer Institute [interested], but I am pleased now that they are moving ahead."[8]

Ironically, both Paulings, despite their vitamin C megadose regimens, died of cancer. Ava Helen's illness and death dealt a severe blow to Pauling and made his later advice to "be happy with your family" quite poignant.

In 1976 Ava Helen was found to have stomach cancer. Pauling never argued that vitamin C therapy was all cancer patients need. In 1991 he said, "we urge that [vitamin C] be taken as an adjunct to appropriate conventional therapy. Do not take it instead of surgery, if it's possible to extricate the cancer."[9] Thus Ava Helen had much of her stomach removed in a gastrectomy.

Pauling also urged patients not to take vitamin C instead of "chemotherapy, if it is a sort of cancer that has been shown definitely to respond to . . . chemotherapy."[10] Despite the advice of cancer experts, however, the Paulings decided Ava Helen would not undergo chemotherapy. Instead, she took a megadose of ten grams of vitamin C daily, as Cameron advised. On this regimen she felt well enough to resume a former interest in piano. She was able to appear at the Monterey, California, chapter of the American Civil Liberties Union on November 1, 1981. There she was honored for her several decades of work defending civil liberties. A few days later, she became very ill. According to Pauling, "[a]n exploratory operation was carried out and it was found that nothing could be done."[11] She died about a month later.

Pauling later spoke with an interviewer about his wife's illness. "[The surgeon] was converted to being a believer in it [vitamin C therapy]. A pretty small fraction of patients with a partial gastrectomy because of stomach cancer survive five years. Probably the vitamin C was responsible for her having most of an additional five years of life. She was active until about a month before her death."[12]

Although Pauling suffered deeply the loss of his wife of fifty-eight years, he eventually resumed a full schedule. He lived on his own. A decade after Ava Helen's death, in December 1991, he was found to have both rectal and prostate cancer. He underwent surgery twice, but otherwise treated himself with vitamin C supplements—first ten, then twelve, then eighteen grams daily. He also followed a diet that emphasized raw fruits, vegetables, and juices. Like Ava Helen, he took painkillers as needed, which was rarely. When people asked him why taking vitamin C hadn't prevented him from getting cancer, he would say, "Perhaps it put it off by twenty years."[13]

After Ava Helen's death, Pauling threw himself into his work. In 1982 he published three papers on the structure of the atomic nucleus. In 1987, now eighty-six, Pauling's publications came out on an average of one every three weeks. When an interviewer asked him if he worked every day, Pauling answered, "Essentially, since my wife died in 1981, I don't have anything else to do."[14] But it was clear that Pauling did the work as much because he thrived on it as to fill his time.

When the interviewer asked Pauling if he had any unfulfilled ambitions, Pauling answered, "I still try to make discoveries. I continue to be interested in orthomolecular medicine and treatment of diseases especially by vitamin C. But I've been spending almost all my time on three problems in physics."[15] In addition to his research on atomic structure, he also published work on superconductivity. (Superconductivity refers to the flow of electric current without resistance through certain materials at very low temperatures.) He also worked on a problem in crystallography that intrigued him.

Interestingly, Pauling continued to do his theoretical

work without a computer. At the lecture he gave at the Caltech symposium in honor of his ninetieth birthday, Pauling said, "Computers do not think. . . . An example of the usefulness of not having a computer is provided by my work during the last six years on [the problem in crystallography]. . . . I made all of the extensive calculations involved in my work without use of a computer, but with use of a small hand calculator." He explained that working this way forced him to think carefully as he made each calculation. As a result, "sometimes during this process I had an idea about how to attack the problem in a somewhat different way." Had he relied on a computer, he was sure, "some of these ideas, which have in fact turned out to be important, would not have occurred to me."[16]

When Pauling became too weak to continue work at the LPI, he spent most of his time at Deer Flat Ranch, the Big Sur country home that he and Ava Helen had bought with the 1954 Nobel prize money. As it became clear that his death was imminent, one of his children was always with him.

Shortly before his death, Pauling attended a meeting of the American Association for the Advancement of Science in San Francisco. Although he arrived in a wheelchair, he managed to walk on his own into the hall where a special symposium was held in his honor. The audience rose as one to its feet as it greeted him with thunderous applause.

Linus Pauling died on August 19, 1994. But his fame did not die with him. In the first few years of the 21st century, people around the world had the opportunity to learn about Pauling's life and work. An exhibition, "Linus Pauling and the 20th Century," was mounted in seven

American and five Japanese cities, where it was viewed by 1.25 million people. It then opened in Paris in March 2003.

Two years after Pauling's death, the Linus Pauling Institute moved to Oregon State University. According to the institute's homepage, "The Institute functions from the basic premise that an optimum diet is the key to optimum health." One of the institute's goals is "to advance knowledge in areas that were of interest to Linus Pauling through research and education."[17] According to Linus Pauling, Jr., his father had fully approved of the move, "to ensure that his research and institute would continue on into the future, for there is very much more to be learned about the relationship of nutrition to health."[18]

Pauling's scientific legacy as a Nobel laureate in chemistry far exceeds his controversial work in nutrition. As one writer put it, "His lasting contribution to science is the profound impact he had on creating a new way of thinking about chemistry and life—the linkage between the inorganic and the organic, among quantum reality, physical chemistry, and . . . disease."[19]

And as long as the drums of war continue to beat around the world, Pauling's legacy as a Nobel peace laureate is also still relevant. His visions of world peace remain a beacon of hope for humanity.

ACTIVITIES

Activity One: Crystal Forms

Linus Pauling made the structure of crystals the subject of his doctoral research. Crystals would also play an important role in Pauling's later research. Crystals make up most non-living substances, including metals, rocks, snowflakes, salt, and sugar.

The shapes of different substances are determined by the way in which their atoms or molecules combine. Most crystals form in stages according to the changing temperatures beneath the earth's surface. First, tremendous heat melts a mass of molecules and atoms. Then, as the mass cools, it takes on a crystalline form. The atoms or molecules of crystals will align themselves in a uniform way at a given temperature. As a result, they create regular geometric patterns. These patterns are symmetrical, which means the pattern can repeat itself in all directions indefinitely. Pauling explained this symmetry by comparing it to the arrangement of bricks in a brick wall. The pattern of bricks repeats in two dimensions. In a crystal, the pattern repeats in three dimensions.

Take some salt crystals and observe them through a magnifying glass or microscope. Try to do this with coarse salt in addition to table salt. What do you see? Rub some of the salt between your fingers. What does it feel like? Take some sugar crystals and do the same. Write down your observations about the different crystals. In what ways are the salt and sugar crystals similar? In what ways are they different?

Snowflakes are composed of crystals. These crystals form out of the water vapor in cold clouds. Snow crystals all have six sides, but they differ in shape. They collide and stick together to produce snowflakes. If the climate and weather permit, you can also observe snowflakes. Write down your observations just as you did with the salt and sugar crystals.

Try to find other crystal forms to observe. Try a nature store or perhaps look for a rock/fossil exhibition. Be sure to bring along your notebook so you can take notes about what you observe. Keep track of what the various crystals have in common and also what their differences are. Think about what makes certain crystals similar and then consider their differences. Do you think the crystals formed under similar or different circumstances? Why? Draw conclusions as to why crystals form in different ways.

Activity Two: Diffraction

Diffraction is the phenomenon displayed by waves (water, sound, light, or any other kind) as they spread out in passing through an opening. Patterns of diffraction can often reveal important information about the diffracting substance. For example, Linus Pauling used X-ray diffraction to discover the molecular structure of many proteins.

In order to understand diffraction better, it might help to see how it actually works. The best way to do so is with a diffraction grating. A diffraction grating is a piece of transparent glass or mirror with lines ruled on it at small, equal intervals. The spaces between the lines are about as far apart as a single wavelength of light. (Visible light waves have wavelengths of less than 1/35,000 of an inch.) Ask your science teacher to obtain a diffraction grating for you. Inexpensive gratings might be an inch across and often come in bundles of twenty to twenty-five, so perhaps your whole class might participate in this activity. Scientists may use gratings twenty centimeters across or greater. A CD also acts as a diffraction grating if you look at the reflection of a light source in some of its shiny parts.

Set up a lamp in the middle of a room and turn it on. View the light from the bulb through your diffraction grating. What do you see? Look through it while holding the grating at various angles. Try circling slowly around the lamp while viewing through the diffraction grating. Now what do you see?

If you view a source of light through a diffraction grating, you should see patterns of different colors. The different colors appear because white light actually consists of different colors, all of them having different wavelengths. A diffraction grating spreads visible light into its component colors. Scientists can identify substances by the pattern of colors they produce through the grating.

Observe other light sources with your diffraction grating. Try to observe candlelight. Go out after sundown and view a mercury streetlight with your diffraction grating, if you can. Other light sources you may try to observe could include a flashlight, Christmas lights, fluorescent ceiling lights, sodium streetlights, and a monitor or television screen.

Which sources of light produce the most similar arrangement of colors? Which sources are the most different? Write down all that you observe. Draw conclusions as to why different light sources produce different patterns of color.

CHRONOLOGY

1901—Linus Pauling is born in Portland, Oregon.

1914—Excitement over a friend's chemistry experiments inspires him to become a chemical engineer.

1917—Leaves Washington High School without a diploma and enters Oregon Agricultural College in Corvallis.

1919–1920—Takes a year off from college to help support his family and becomes interested in the chemical bond.

1922—Earns his undergraduate degree in chemical engineering and becomes a graduate student at the California Institute of Technology in Pasadena.

1923—Marries Ava Helen Miller.

1925—Receives his doctorate in chemistry and becomes a father to the first of his four children.

1926–1927—Studies quantum mechanics in Europe as a Guggenheim Fellow.

1927—Joins the faculty of Caltech.

1931—Becomes a full professor at Caltech and publishes his first paper on the nature of the chemical bond.

1934—Begins his research in biochemistry.

1937—Becomes chairman of Caltech's division of chemistry and chemical engineering.

1939—His *The Nature of the Chemical Bond and the Structure of Molecules and Crystals* is published.

1940—Strictly follows an experimental diet as treatment for an often fatal kidney disease.

1941–1945—Does research related to the war effort.

1946—Becomes involved in activism against the nuclear bomb.

1947—Publishes an important college textbook, *General Chemistry.*

1949—Publishes a paper that identifies sickle-cell anemia as the first molecular disease.

1951—Publishes papers on the alpha helix, which he identifies as a structural feature of many proteins.

1952—The State Department refuses to grant him a passport.

1952–1953—Incorrectly identifies the triple helix as the basic structure of DNA.

1954—Wins the Nobel Prize for chemistry for his work on the chemical bond.

1956–1961—Focuses on political activism, speaking out about the danger of nuclear fallout.

1958—Publishes *No More War!*; delivers to the secretary general of the United Nations a petition signed by thousands of scientists from around the world calling for an end to nuclear testing, and is forced to resign as division chairman at Caltech.

1960—Withholds from a Senate subcommittee the names of those who helped him circulate the anti-testing petition.

1963—Wins the Nobel Peace Prize immediately after the first nuclear test-ban treaty is put into effect and resigns his position at Caltech.

1964–1967—Serves as a research fellow at the Center for the Study of Democratic Institutions in Santa Barbara, California.

1966—Becomes interested in the use of vitamin C megadoses to prevent disease.

1967–1969—Serves as research professor of chemistry at the University of California at San Diego.

1969–1974—Serves as professor of chemistry at Stanford University in Palo Alto, California.

1970—Publishes *Vitamin C and the Common Cold,* which becomes a bestseller.

1973—Cofounds with Arthur Robinson a research institute devoted to "orthomolecular medicine," which in 1974 is named the Linus Pauling Institute of Science and Medicine.

1979—Publishes with Ewan Cameron *Vitamin C and Cancer.*

1981—Ava Helen Pauling dies of stomach cancer.

1986—Publishes *How to Live Longer and Feel Better.*

1991—Learns that he has prostate and rectal cancer.

1994—Dies of cancer on August 19.

1996—The Linus Pauling Institute moves to Oregon State University.

2001–2003—The exhibit "Linus Pauling and the 20th Century" is viewed in the U.S., Japan, and France.

CHAPTER NOTES

Chapter 1. A Laureate Respected and Reviled

1. Barbara Marinacci, ed., *Linus Pauling in His Own Words: Selections From His Writings, Speeches, and Interviews* (New York: Touchstone, 1995), p. 134.

2. Richard Severo, "Linus C. Pauling Dies at 93: Chemist and Voice for Peace," *The New York Times*, August 21, 1994, p. 1.

3. Marinacci, op. cit., pp. 171–178.

4. Clifford Mead and Thomas Hager, eds., *Linus Pauling: Scientist and Peacemaker* (Corvallis: Oregon State University Press, 2001), p. 236.

5. Derek A. Davenport, "The Many Lives of Linus Pauling: A Review of Reviews," *Journal of Chemical Education*, vol. 73, No. 9, September 1996, p. A212.

Chapter 2. An Oregon Boyhood

1. Linus Pauling, "Starting Out," *Linus Pauling in His Own Words: Selections From His Writings, Speeches, and Interviews*, ed. Barbara Marinacci (New York: Touchstone, 1995), p. 26.

2. Ibid., p. 27.

3. Ibid., p. 26.

4. Ibid., p. 34.

5. Linus Pauling, "An Extraordinary Life: An Autobiographical Ramble," *Creativity: Paradoxes and Reflections,* ed. Harry A. Wilmer (Wilmette, Ill: Chiron Publications, 1991), p. 69.

6. Linus Pauling, "How I Developed an Interest in the Question of the Nature of Life," *Linus Pauling: Scientist and Peacemaker*, eds. Clifford Mead and Thomas Hager (Corvallis: Oregon University Press, 2001), p. 135.

7. Linus Pauling, "How I Became Interested in the Chemical Bond: A Reminiscence," *The Chemical Bond: Structure and Dynamics*, ed. Ahmed Zewail (San Diego: Academic Press, 1992), p. 99.

8. Marinacci, op. cit., p. 30.

9. Linus Pauling, "Fifty Years of Progress in Structural Chemistry and Molecular Biology," *Daedalus 99*, Fall 1970, p. 988.

10. Wilmer, op. cit., p. 70.

11. Mead and Hager, op. cit., p. 21.

12. Marinacci, op. cit., p. 32.

13. Ibid.

14. Mead and Hager, op. cit., p. 27.

15. Marinacci, op. cit., p. 33.

16. Ibid.

17. Ibid., p. 34.

18. Ibid.

19. Ibid., p. 33.

20. Mead and Hager, op. cit., p. 22.

21. Ibid., p. 22.

22. Mead and Hager, op. cit., p. 25.

Chapter 3. Undergraduate Years

1. Linus Pauling, "An Extraordinary Life: An Autobiographical Ramble," *Creativity: Paradoxes and Reflections*, ed. Harry A. Wilmer (Wilmette, Ill.: Chiron Publications, 1991), p. 77.

2. Linus Pauling, "Starting Out," *Linus Pauling in His Own Words: Selections From His Writings, Speeches, and Interviews*, ed. Barbara Marinacci (New York: Touchstone, 1995), p. 34.

3. Clifford Mead and Thomas Hager, eds., *Linus Pauling; Scientist and Peacemaker* (Corvallis: Oregon State University Press, 2001), p. 29.

4. Marinacci, op. cit., p. 35.

5. Linus Pauling, "How My Interest in Proteins Developed," *Protein Science*, 1993.

6. Marinacci, op. cit., p. 35.

7. Ibid., p. 36.

8. Ibid.

9. Wilmer, op. cit., p. 75.

10. Linus Pauling, "Fifty Years of Progress in Structural Chemistry and Molecular Biology," *Daedalus 99*, Fall 1970, p. 990.

11. Ibid., p. 994.

12. Marinacci, op. cit., p. 37.

13. Linus Pauling, "Fifty Years of Progress in Structural Chemistry and Molecular Biology," p. 988.

14. Mead and Hager, op. cit., p. 36.

15. Thomas Hager, *Force of Nature: The Life of Linus Pauling* (New York: Simon and Schuster, 1995), p. 66.

16. Marinacci, op. cit., p. 42.

17. Hager, op. cit., p. 55.

18. Marinacci, op. cit., p. 41.

19. Ted Goertzel and Ben Goertzel, *Linus Pauling: A Life in Science and Politics* (New York: Basic Books, 1995), p. 32.

20. Marinacci, op. cit., p. 40.

21. Linus Pauling, "Fifty Years of Physical Chemistry in the California Institute of Technology," *Annual Review of Physical Chemistry*, no. 16 (1965), p. 2.

22. Hager, op. cit., p. 73.

Chapter 4. Pasadena and Europe

1. Linus Pauling, "Fifty Years of Physical Chemistry in the California Institute of Technology," *Annual Review of Physical Chemistry*, no. 16 (1965), p. 2.

2. Clifford Mead and Thomas Hager, eds., *Linus Pauling: Scientist and Peacemaker* (Corvallis: Oregon State University Press, 2001), p. 32.

3. Linus Pauling, "An Extraordinary Life: An Autobiographical Ramble," *Creativity: Paradoxes and Reflections*, ed. Harry A. Wilmer (Wilmette, Ill: Chiron Publications, 1991), p. 73.

4. Linus Pauling, "X-Ray Crystallography and the Nature of the Chemical Bond," *The Chemical Bond: Structure and Dynamics*, ed. Ahmed Zewail (San Diego: Academic Press, 1992), pp. 5, 7.

5. Wilmer, op. cit., p. 73.

6. Linus Pauling, "Fifty Years of Progress in Structural Chemistry and Molecular Biology," *Daedalus 99*, Fall 1970, pp. 991–992.

7. Linus Pauling, "How I Developed an Interest in the Question of the Nature of Life," Mead and Hager, op. cit., p. 137.

8. Ibid., p. 32.

9. Wilmer, op. cit., p. 69.

10. Judith R. Goodstein, "Atoms, Molecules, and Linus Pauling," *Social Research*, Autumn 1984, vol. 51, no. 3, p. 697.

11. Thomas Hager, *Force of Nature: The Life of Linus Pauling* (New York: Simon and Schuster, 1995), p. 105.

12. "Probing the Chemical Bond," *Linus Pauling in His Own Words: Selections From His Writings, Speeches, and Interviews*, ed. Barbara Marinacci (New York: Touchstone, 1995), p. 71.

13. Ibid., p. 72.

14. Linus Pauling, "Fifty Years of Progress in Structural Chemistry and Molecular Biology," *Daedalus 99*, Fall 1970, p. 993.

15. Hager, op. cit., p. 121.

16. Ibid., p. 129.

17. Denis Brian, "Linus Pauling," *Genius Talk: Conversations with Nobel Scientists and Other Luminaries* (New York: Plenum Press, 1995), p. 4.

18. Goodstein, op. cit., pp. 700-701.

19. Linus Pauling, "How I Became Interested in the Chemical Bond: A Reminiscence," Zewail, op. cit., pp. 107–108.

20. Marinacci, op. cit., p. 72.

Chapter 5. Bridging Chemistry and Physics

1. Judith R. Goodstein, *Millikan's School: A History of the California Institute of Technology* (New York and London: W. W. Norton & Company, 1991), p. 186.

2. Linus Pauling, "An Extraordinary Life: An Autobiographical Ramble," *Creativity: Paradoxes and Reflections*, ed. Harry A. Wilmer (Wilmette, Ill.: Chiron Publications, 1991), p. 69.

3. Ibid.

4. Anthony Serafini, *Linus Pauling: A Man and His Science* (New York: Paragon House, 1989), p. 53.

5. Thomas Hager, *Force of Nature: The Life of Linus Pauling* (New York: Simon & Schuster, 1995), p. 142.

6. Ibid., p. 156–157.

7. Clifford Mead and Thomas Hager, eds., *Linus Pauling: Scientist and Peacemaker* (Corvallis: Oregon State University Press, 2001), p. 35.

8. Ibid., p. 110.

9. Ibid., op. cit., p. 83.

10. Ibid., p. 256.

11. Rae Goodell, *The Visible Scientists* (Boston and Toronto: Little, Brown and Company, 1977), p. 87.

12. E-mail correspondence between author and Jenny Munn, National Academy of Sciences, February 7, 2003.

13. Alexander Rich and Norman Davidson, eds., *Structural Chemistry and Molecular Biology* (San Francisco and London: W. H. Freeman and Company, 1968), p. iv.

14. Mead and Hager, op. cit., p. 69.

15. Dudley R. Herschbach, "Chemical Reaction Dynamics and Electronic Structure," *The Chemical Bond: Structure and Dynamics*, Ahmed Zewail, ed., (San Diego: Academic Press, 1992), p. 176.

16. John W. Servos, *Physical Chemistry from Ostwald to Pauling: The Making of a Science in America* (Princeton: Princeton University Press, 1990), p. 296.

17. Judith R. Goodstein, *Millikan's School: A History of the California Institute of Technology* (New York and London: W. W. Norton & Company, 1991), p. 192.

18. Linus Pauling, "Fifty Years of Physical Chemistry in the California Institute of Technology," *Annual Review of Physical Chemistry*, 1965, p. 3.

19. Anthony Serafini, *Linus Pauling: A Man and His Science* (New York: Paragon House, 1989), p. 103.

20. Servos, op. cit., p. 297.

21. Rich, op. cit., p. iv.

22. Linus Pauling, "Fifty Years of Progress in Structural Chemistry and Molecular Biology," *Daedalus 99*, Fall 1970, p. 998.

Chapter 6. Bridging Chemistry, Biology, and Medicine

1. "Molecular Biology," *World Book Encyclopedia*, 2001, s.v., p. 692.

2. Thomas Hager, *Force of Nature: The Life of Linus Pauling* (New York: Simon & Schuster, 1995), p. 188.

3. Linus Pauling, "Fifty Years of Progress in Structural Chemistry and Molecular Biology," Gerald Holton, ed., *The 20th-century Sciences: Studies in the Biography of Ideas* (New York: Norton, 1972), p. 295.

4. Ibid., p. 296.

5. Hager, op. cit., p. 323.

6. Ibid., p. 324.

7. Ibid., p.379.

8. James D. Watson, *The Double Helix: A Personal Account of the Discovery of the Structure of DNA* (New York: Atheneum, 1968), p. 78.

9. Ibid., p. 48.

10. Ibid., p. 77.

11. Ibid., p. 160.

12. Ibid., p. 161.

13. Ibid., p. 161.

14. Ibid., p. 170.

15. Hager, op. cit., p. 428.

16. Linus Pauling, "An Extraordinary Life: An Autobiographical Ramble," Harry A. Wilmer, ed., *Creativity: Paradoxes and Reflections* (Wilmette, Ill: Chiron Publications, 1991), p. 78.

Chapter 7. Patriot or Traitor?

1. Thomas Hager, *Force of Nature: The Life of Linus Pauling* (New York: Simon & Schuster, 1995), p. 259.

2. "Linus Pauling—Scientist for the Ages," March 18, 2003, <http://lpi.oregonstate.edu/lpbio/lpbio2.html> (May 9, 2003).

3. Clifford Mead and Thomas Hager, eds., *Linus Pauling: Scientist and Peacemaker* (Corvallis: Oregon State University Press, 2001), p. 37.

4. Barbara Marinacci, ed., *Linus Pauling in His Own Words: Selections from His Writings, Speeches, and Interviews* (New York: Touchstone, 1995), p. 152.

5. Mead and Hager, op. cit., pp. 192–194.

6. Ibid., p. 13.

7. Ibid., p. 44.

8. Ibid., p. 51.

9. Ted Goertzel and Ben Goertzel, *Linus Pauling: A Life in Science and Politics* (New York: Basic Books, 1995), p. 144.

10. Marinacci, op. cit., p. 180.

11. Linda Pauling Kamb, email communication with author, February 18, 2003.

12. Marinacci, op. cit., p. 12.

13. Ibid., p. 181.

14. George B. Kauffman and Laurie M. Kauffman, "Linus Pauling: Reflections," *American Scientist*, November 1994, no. 82, p. 524.

Chapter 8. In Search of a New Home

1. Barbara Marinacci, ed., *Linus Pauling in His Own Words: Selections from His Writings, Speeches, and Interviews* (New York: Touchstone, 1995), p. 12.

2. Clifford Mead and Thomas Hager, eds., *Linus Pauling: Scientist and Peacemaker* (Corvallis: Oregon State University Press, 2001), p. 45.

3. Ibid., 45.

4. Ibid., p. 45.

5. Denis Brian, *Genius Talk: Conversations with Nobel Scientists and Other Luminaries* (New York: Plenum Press, 1995), p. 11.

6. Ibid., 13.

7. Ibid., p. 13.

8. Thomas Hager, *Force of Nature: The Life of Linus Pauling* (New York: Simon & Schuster, 1995), p. 556.

9. Ibid., p. 569.

10. Marc Abrahams, "Ig Nobel Prize Update," n.d., <http://web.mit.edu/afs/athena.mit.edu/activity/v/voodoo/www/is743/ignoble.html> (May 9, 2003).

11. Linus Pauling, *Vitamin C and the Common Cold* (San Francisco: W. H. Freeman, 1970), pp. 4, 5, 6.

Chapter 9. Industrious to the End

1. Linus Pauling, *How to Live Longer and Feel Better* (New York: Freeman, 1986), p. 9.

2. Luther J. Carter, "Pauling Gets Medal of Science: Thaw Between Scientists and White House," *Science*, October 3, 1975, p.33.

3. Rae Goodell, *The Visible Scientists* (Boston and Toronto: Little, Brown and Company, 1977), p. 79.

4. Clifford Mead and Thomas Hager, eds., *Linus Pauling: Scientist and Peacemaker* (Corvallis: Oregon State University Press, 2001), p. 235.

5. Ahmed Zewail, ed., *The Chemical Bond: Structure and Dynamics* (San Diego: Academic Press, 1992), p. xiii.

6. Thomas Hager, *Force of Nature: The Life of Linus Pauling* (New York: Simon & Schuster, 1995), p. 607.

7. Ibid., p. 617.

8. Mead and Hager, op. cit., p. 47.

9. Linus Pauling, "An Extraordinary Life: An Autobiographical Ramble," Harry A. Wilmer, ed., *Creativity: Paradoxes and Reflections* (Wilmette, Ill.: Chiron Publications, 1991), p. 82.

10. Ibid., p. 82.

11. Denis Brian, "Linus Pauling," *Conversations with Nobel Scientists and Other Luminaries* (New York: Plenum Press, 1995), p. 19.

12. Ibid., p. 19.

13. Ibid., p. 20.

14. Ibid.,p. 29.

15. Ibid., p. 22.

16. Linus Pauling, "X-Ray Crystallography and the Nature of the Chemical Bond," Zewail, op. cit., pp. 8, 10–11.

17. *The Linus Pauling Institute*, n.d., <http://www.lpi.oregonstate.edu> (May 9, 2003).

18. Linus Pauling, Jr., "A Message From Linus Pauling, Jr.," Spring/Summer 1997, <http://lpi.oregonstate.edu/sp-su97/junior.html> (May 9, 2003).

19. Mark S. Lesney, "Pauling, Linus Carl," *American National Biography*, eds. John A. Garraty and Mark C. Carnes (New York and Oxford: Oxford University Press, 1999), vol. 17, p. 168.

GLOSSARY

alpha helix—The spiral-shaped feature that Pauling determined was the fundamental structural element of keratin.

amino acid—The building block of protein.

antibody—A protein substance produced in the blood or tissues in response to a specific antigen.

antigen—A substance that, when introduced into the body, stimulates the production of an antibody.

ascorbic acid—Vitamin C.

atom—A unit of matter consisting of a dense, central, positively charged nucleus surrounded by negatively charged electrons.

biochemistry—The study of the chemical substances and vital processes occurring in living organisms.

blood plasma—The fluid portion of the blood.

capitalism—Economic system in which the means of production and distribution are privately or corporately owned.

chemical bond—Any of several forces or mechanisms by which atoms are bound in a molecule or crystal.

chemistry—The science of the composition, structure, properties, and reactions of matter.

Cold War—The intense post-World War II rivalry between the Soviet Union and its Communist allies and the United States and its democratic allies.

communism—A system of government in which the state plans and controls the economy and a single, often dictatorial party holds power, claiming to aspire toward a social order in which the people share all goods equally.

crystal—A solid formed by a repeating, three-dimensional pattern of atoms or molecules and having fixed distances between constituent parts.

denaturation—Alteration of the structure of a protein so that some of its original properties are diminished or destroyed.

Depression—Economic slump in North America, Europe, and other industrialized areas of the world that began in 1929 and lasted until after the United States' entry into World War II.

DNA—The molecule found in all living cells that codes genetic information for the transmission of inherited traits.

electron—Negatively charged subatomic particle that plays a vital role in the formation of the chemical bonds that account for the association of atoms into molecules and crystals.

electron diffraction—Bending of a beam of electrons when passing near matter; by interpreting the patterns that are formed when parts of the diffracted electron beam cross each other, scientists can identify a substance chemically or locate the position of atoms in a substance.

entomology—The scientific study of insects.

experimentalist—Scientist who collects and interprets data to determine how substances behave.

fallout—Radioactive particles that descend in the atmosphere after a nuclear explosion.

genetics—The branch of biology that deals with heredity.

hemoglobin—A complex molecule, including iron and the protein globin, that transports oxygen in the blood and gives blood its red color.

inorganic chemistry—Chemistry of nonliving things.

keratin—Protein substance making up hair, nails, horns, and hoofs.

Manhattan Project—U.S. government research project (1942-45) that produced the first atomic bombs.

megadose—An exceptionally large dose of a vitamin or drug.

mineral—Naturally occurring solid with a characteristic crystalline structure.

molecular biology—The branch of biology that deals with the formation, structure, and activity of the large molecules essential to life, such as nucleic acids and proteins.

"molecular complementariness"—Term Pauling used to explain that biological processes depended on the precise fit of one molecule against or into another molecule with a shape complementary to it.

molecular disease—Disease such as sickle cell anemia that is caused by a flaw in the structure of a molecule.

molecule—A group of atoms held together by chemical forces.

nucleic acid—The genetic material of living cells, which controls heredity.

nucleus—The core of an atom.

organic chemistry—The chemistry of carbon compounds.

orthomolecular—Term used by Pauling to assert that optimal health depends on the proper levels of chemical substances, such as vitamins, in the body.

peacenik—Informal term for a political activist who publicly opposes war or the proliferation of weapons.

peptide—Compound containing linked amino acids.

pernicious anemia—Severe deficiency in the blood's ability to carry oxygen, characterized by abnormally large red blood cells, caused by failure of the stomach to absorb vitamin B-12.

physical chemistry—Scientific analysis of the properties and behavior of chemical systems from a physicist's perspective.

physics—The science of matter and energy and of interactions between the two.

polypeptide—Peptide containing more than three amino acids.

protein—Fundamental component of all living cells, composed of one or more chains of amino acids.

quantum mechanics—Refinements of quantum theory, developed in the 1920s, to describe the structure and behavior of atoms and molecules.

quantum theory—A mathematical method describing how matter worked on the atomic level, developed in the early 20th century, that called into question many long-held ideas about physics.

RDA—Recommended daily allowance established by the U.S. government for intake of vitamins.

resonance—Pauling's theory that some molecules, such as benzene, cannot be described accurately in terms of a single structure and must be described as fluctuating, or resonating, between two or more structures at the same time.

royalties—Payments from publishing companies to authors from the proceeds of the sales of their books.

sickle cell anemia—Chronic anemia marked by crescent-shaped red blood cells.

silicate—Any of a large group of minerals that form over 90 percent of the earth's crust.

stereochemistry—Branch of chemistry dealing with the spatial arrangements of atoms in molecules and their effect on the properties of matter.

structural chemistry—The branch of chemistry that studies the structure, or three-dimensional geometry, of molecules or solids.

superconductivity—The flow of electric current without resistance in certain materials at very low temperatures.

theoretician—A scientist who works out theories to explain why matter behaves as it does.

vitamin—Substance obtained from plant and animal foods that is essential for normal growth and activity of the body.

wave mechanics—A form of quantum mechanics.

X-ray crystallography—The study of crystal structure by means of X-ray diffraction.

X-ray diffraction—The scattering of X-rays by crystal atoms, producing a pattern that yields information about the structure of the crystal.

FURTHER READING

Hager, Tom. *Linus Pauling and the Chemistry of Life*. New York: Oxford University Press, Inc., 1998.

Newton, David E. *Linus Pauling: Scientist and Advocate*. New York: Facts on File, 1994.

Pasachoff, Naomi. *Niels Bohr: Physicist and Humanitarian*. Berkeley Heights, N.J.: Enslow Publishers, Inc., 2003.

Richards, Jon. *Chemicals & Reactions*. Brookfield, Conn.: Millbrook Press, Inc., 2000.

Sherrow, Victoria. *Linus Pauling: Investigating the Magic Within*. Orlando, Fla.: Raintree Steck-Vaughn Publishers, 1997.

Tiner, John Hudson. *Exploring the World of Chemistry*. Green Forest, Ark.: Master Books, 2000.

Zannos, Susan. *Linus Pauling and the Chemical Bond*. Bear, Del.: Mitchell Lane Publishers, 2002.

INTERNET ADDRESSES

Linus Pauling Institute (LPI)
http://www.orst.edu/dept/lpi/

Linus Pauling and the Twentieth Century: An Exhibition
http://www.paulingexhibit.org

Nobel e-Museum
http://www.nobel.se/

INDEX